Art by L. Chenault from 2001-2015

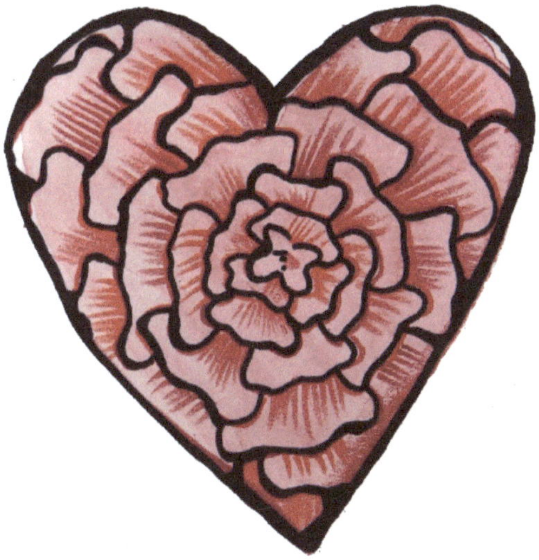

ISBN:1522759980
ISBN-13:9781522759980

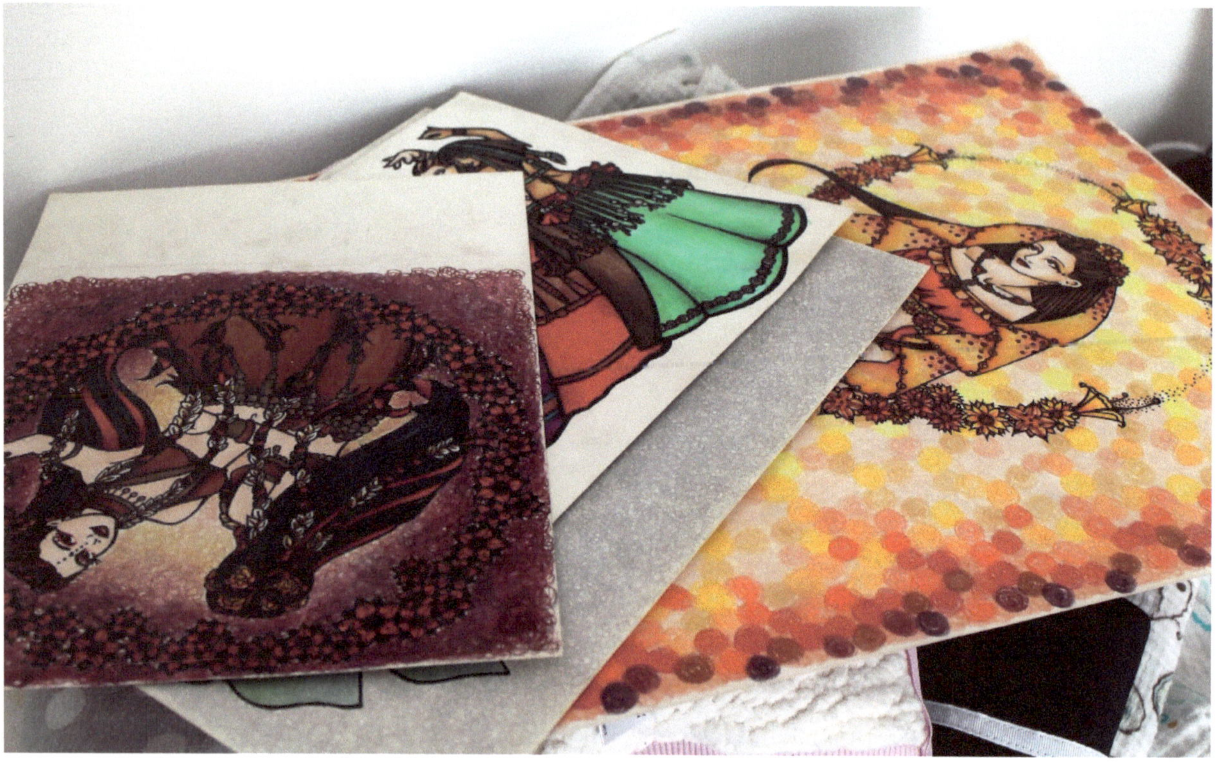

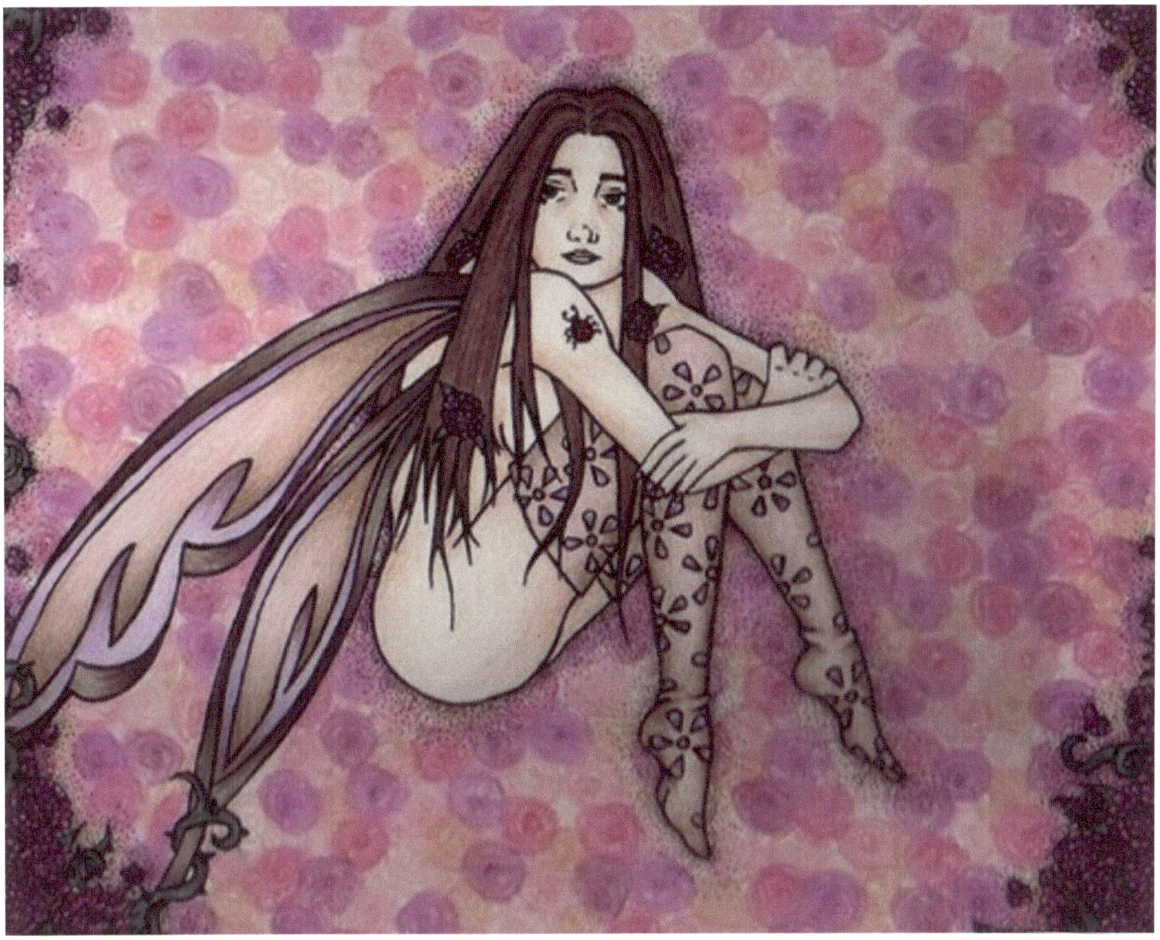

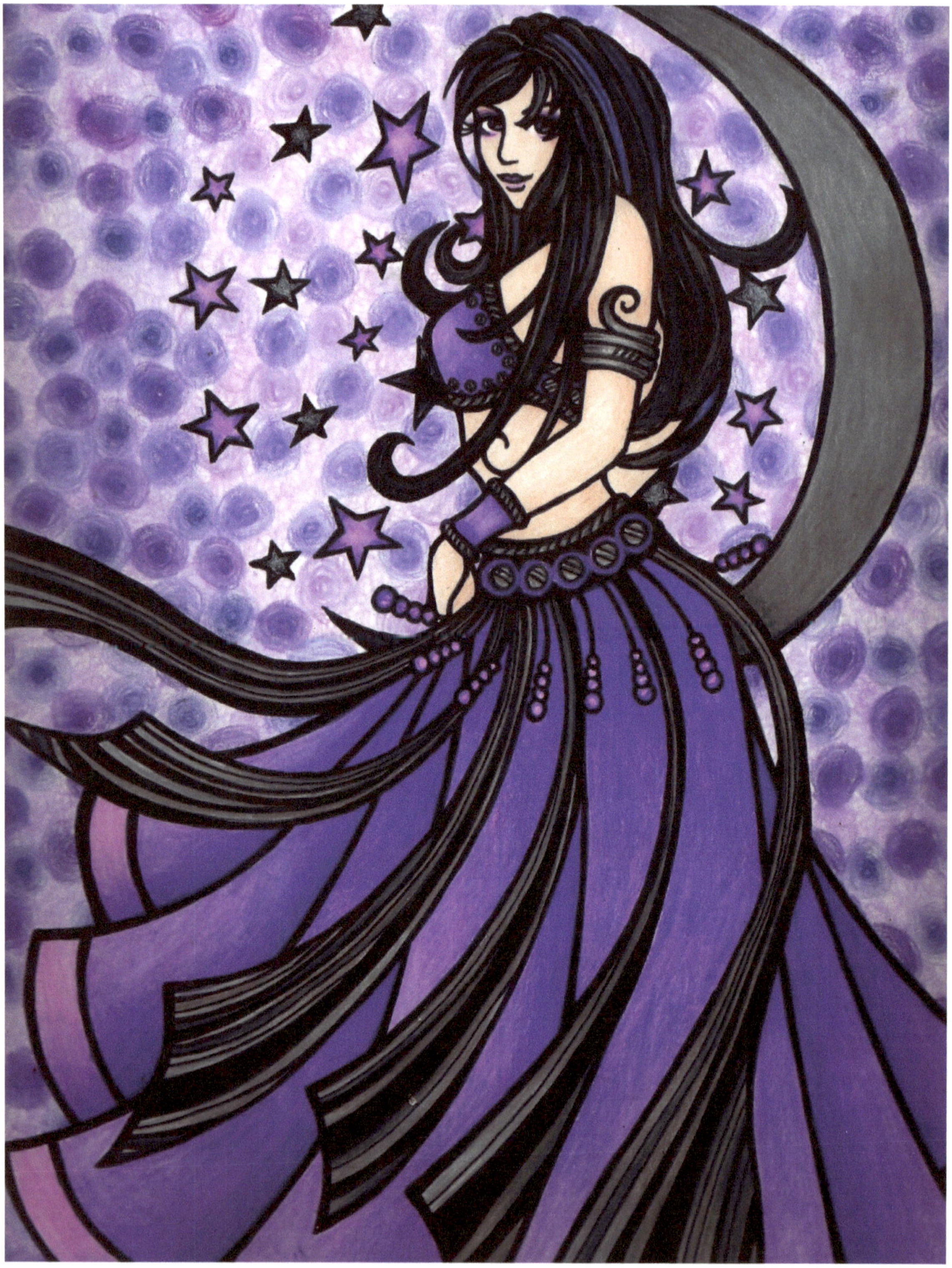

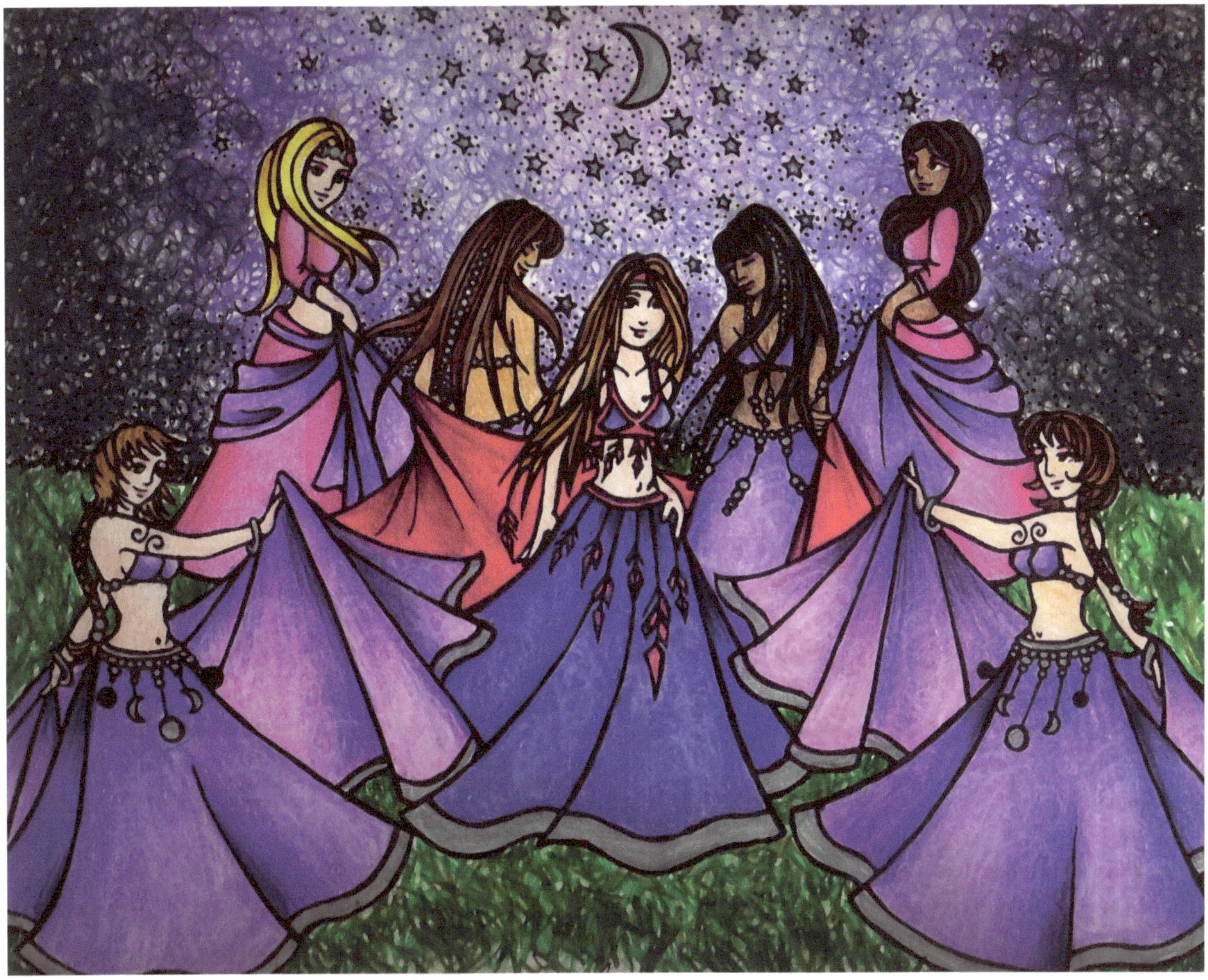

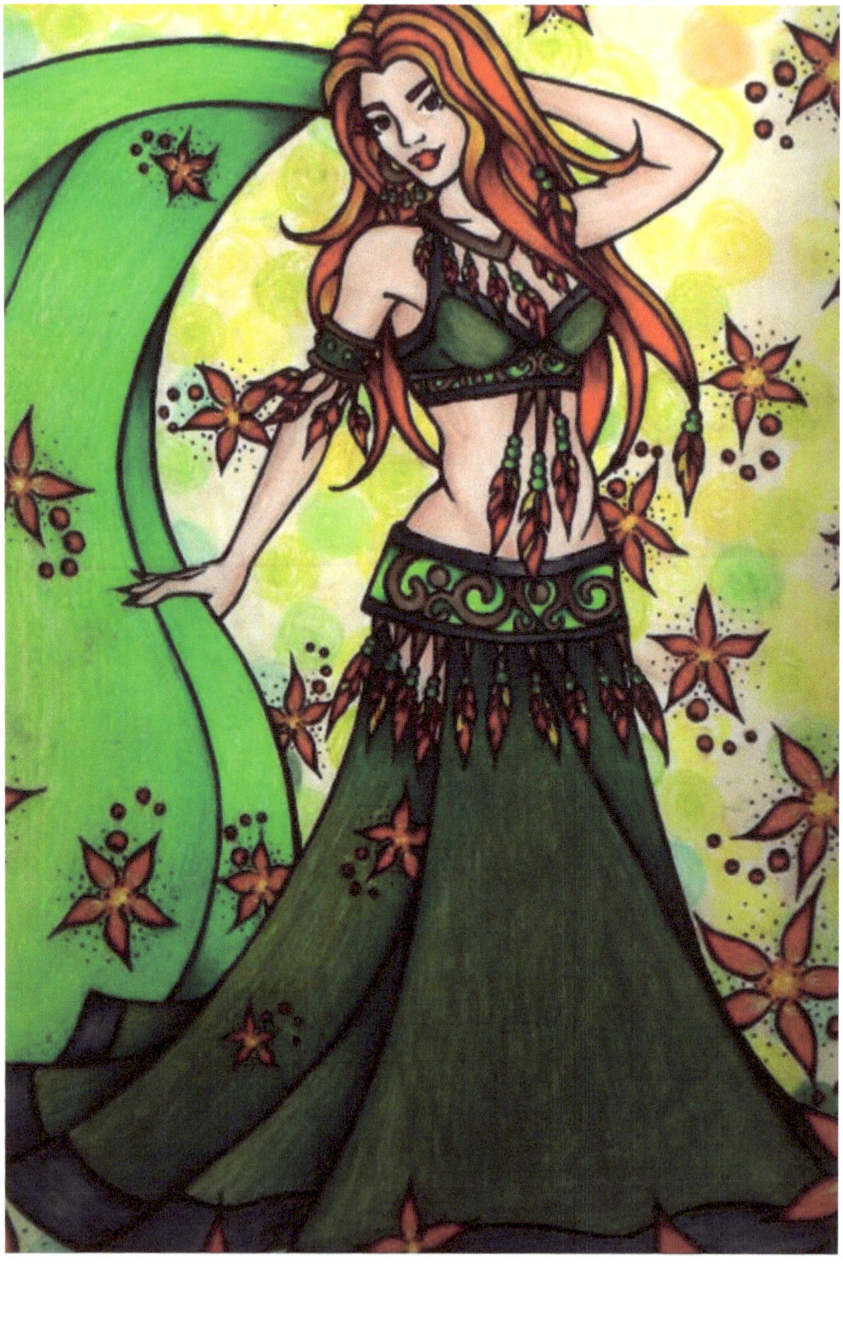

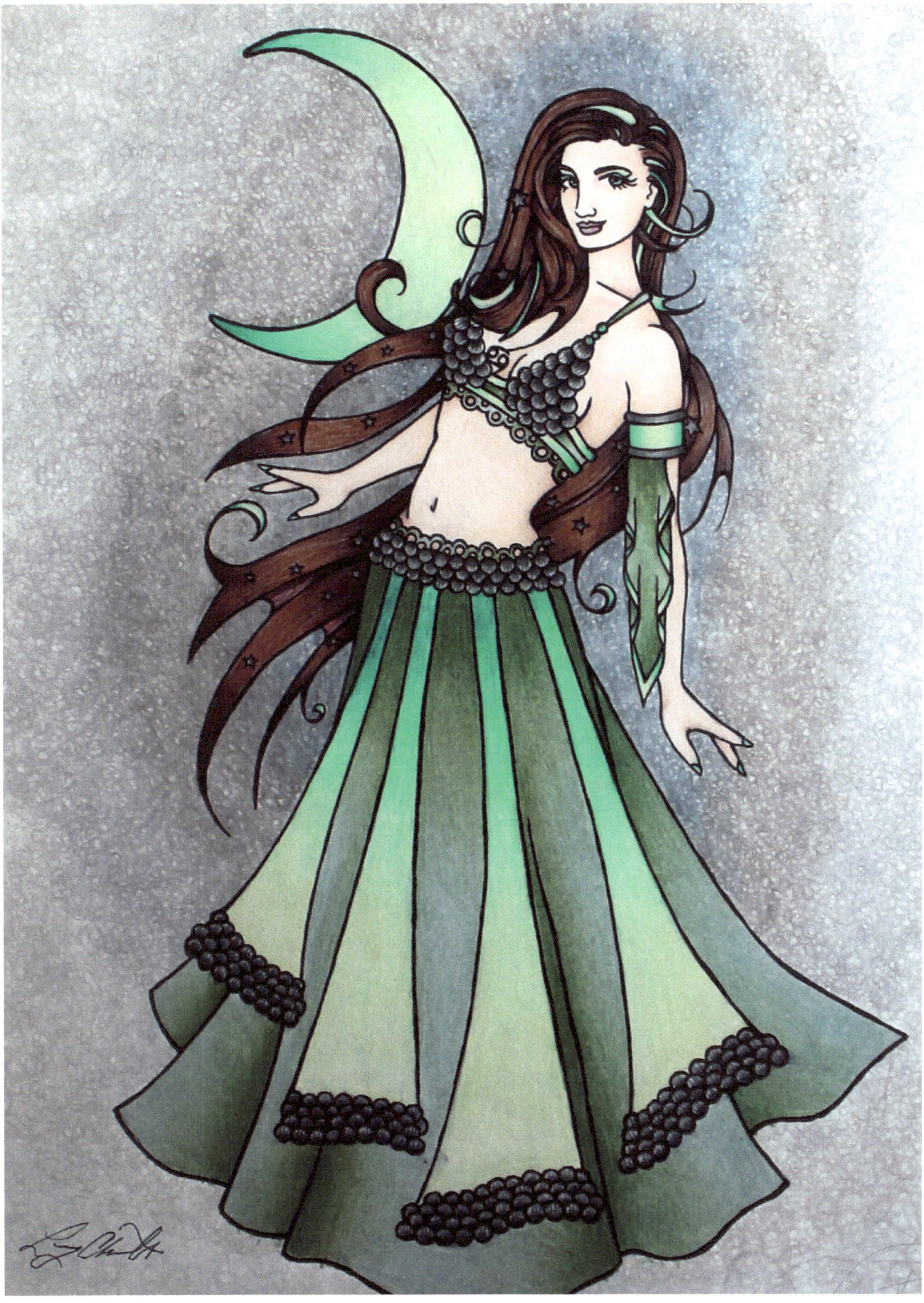

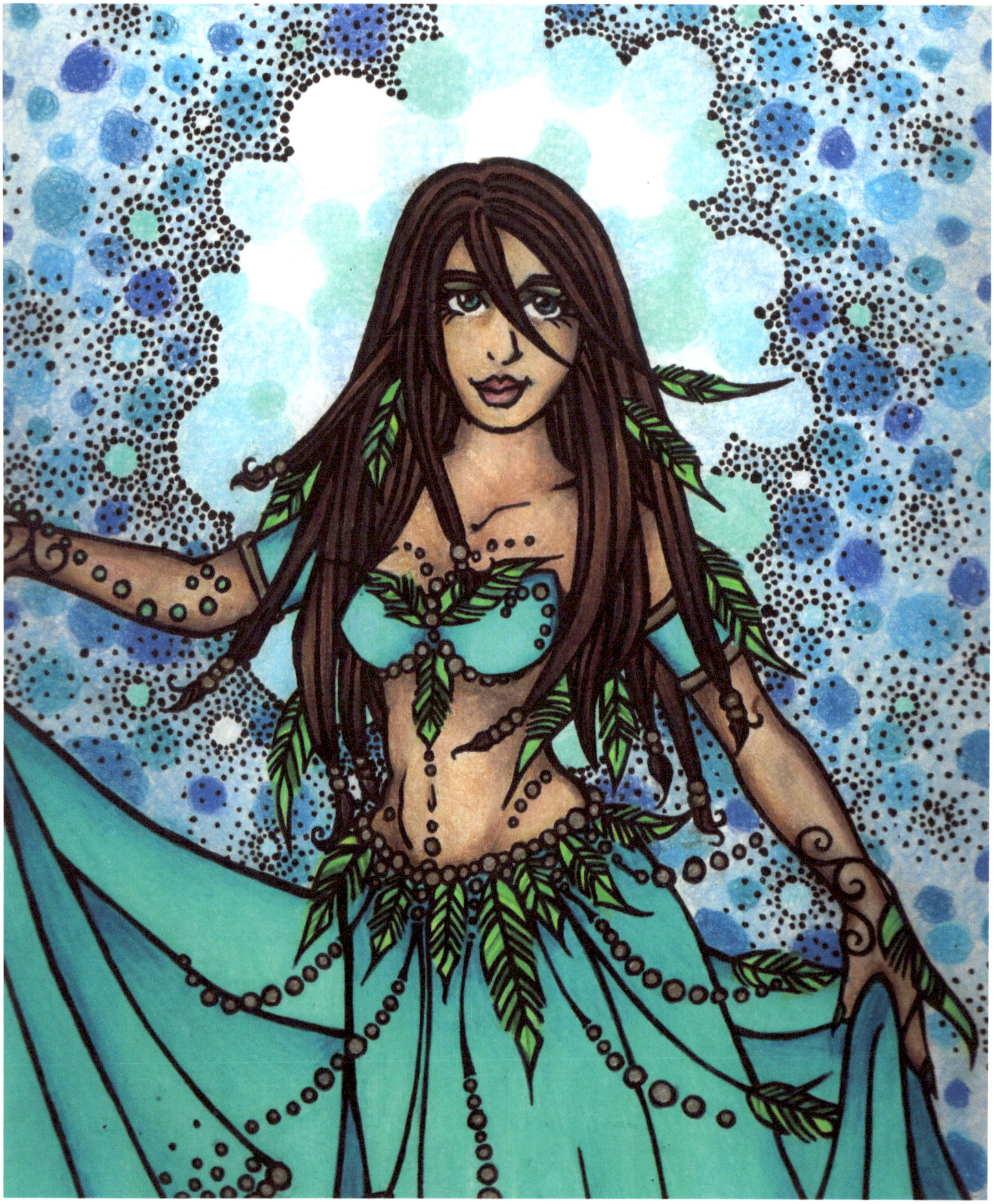

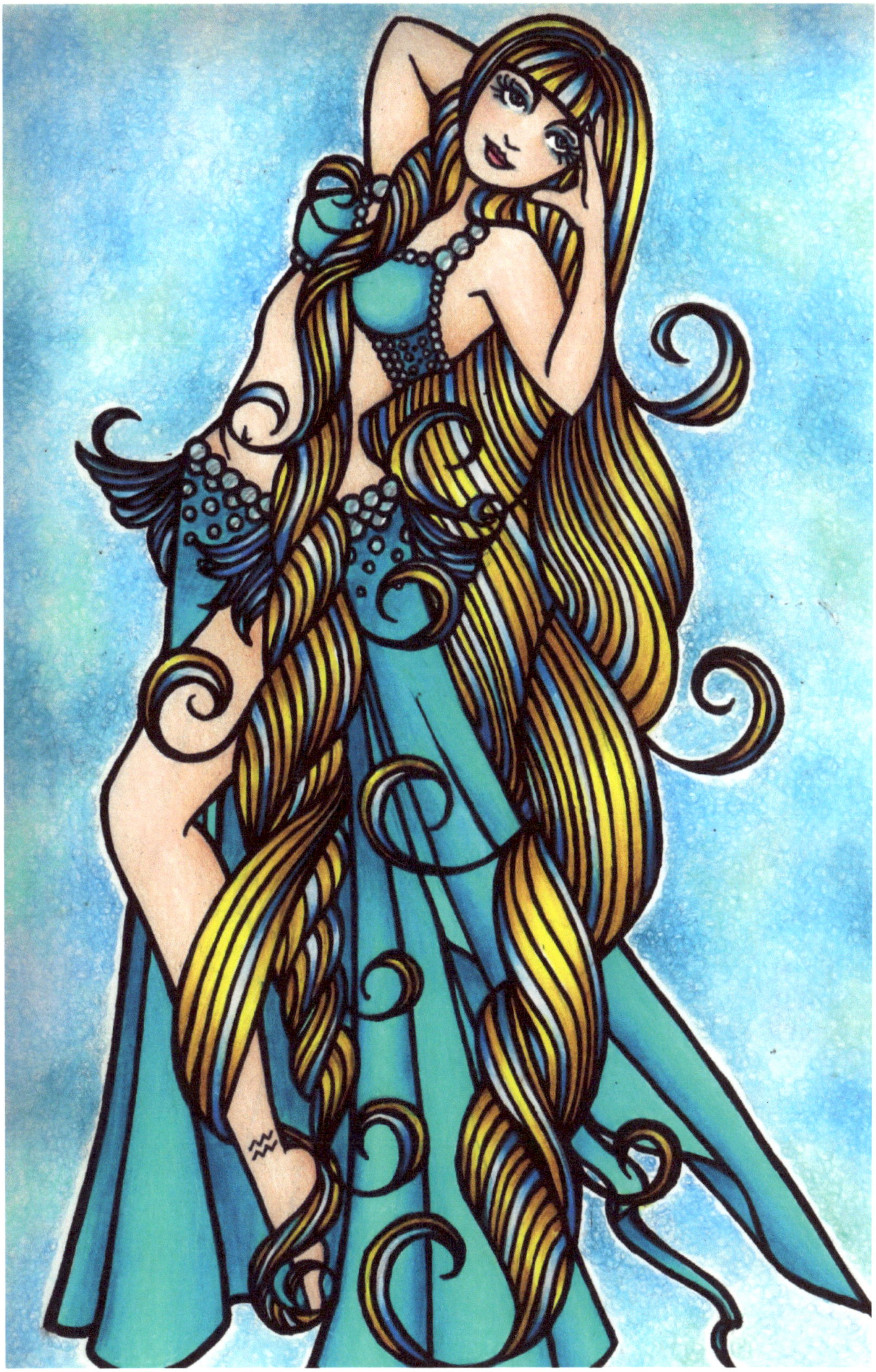

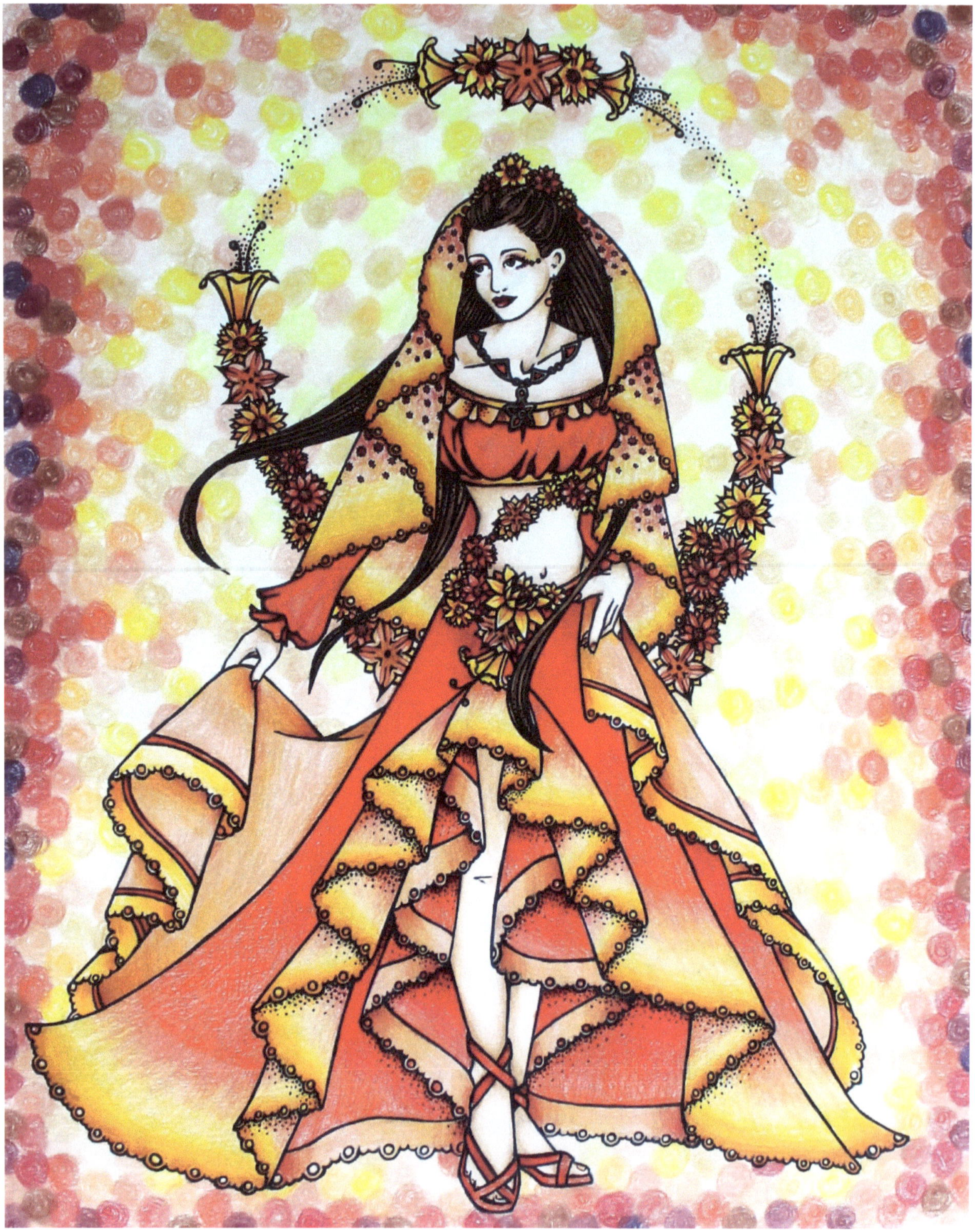

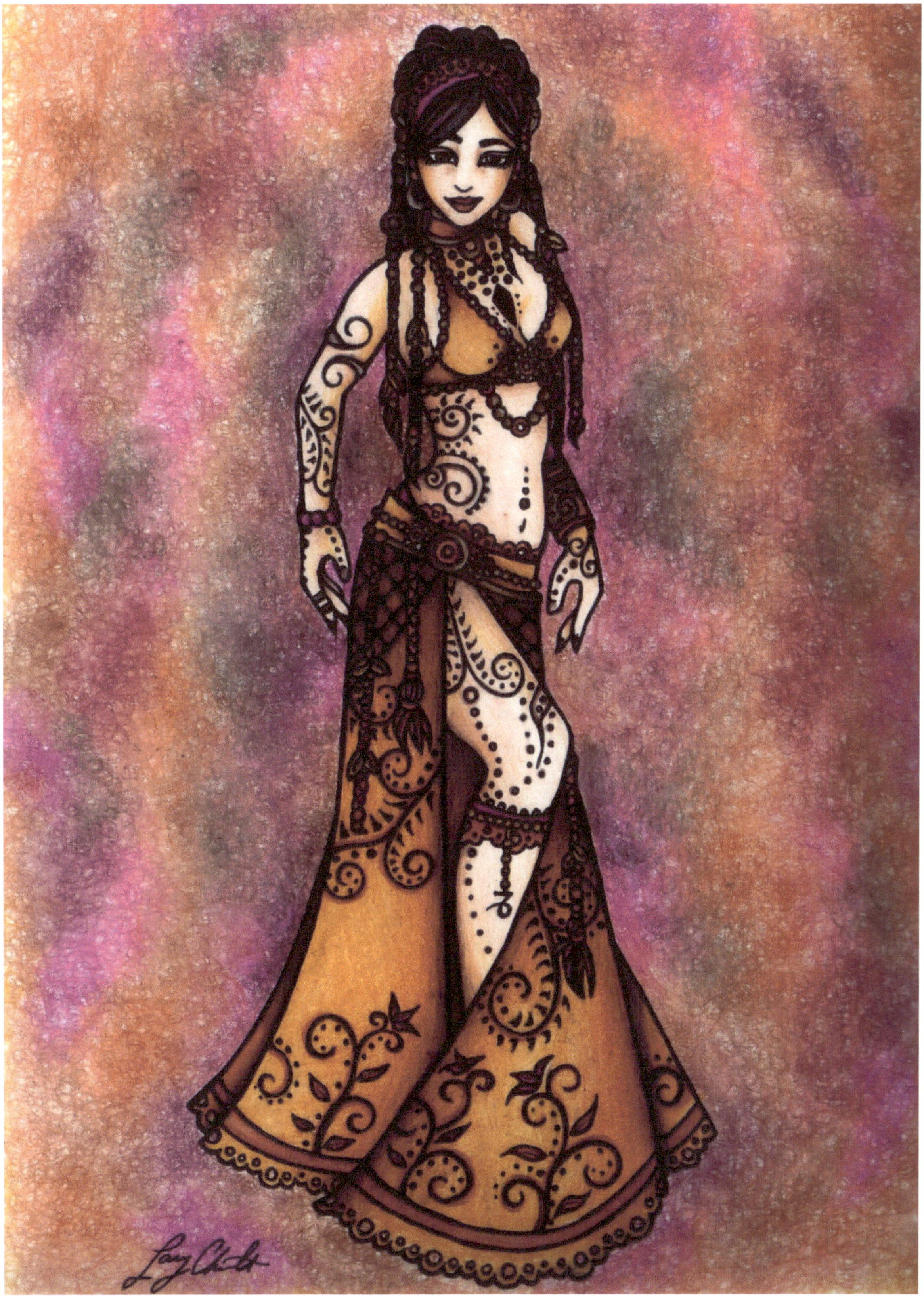

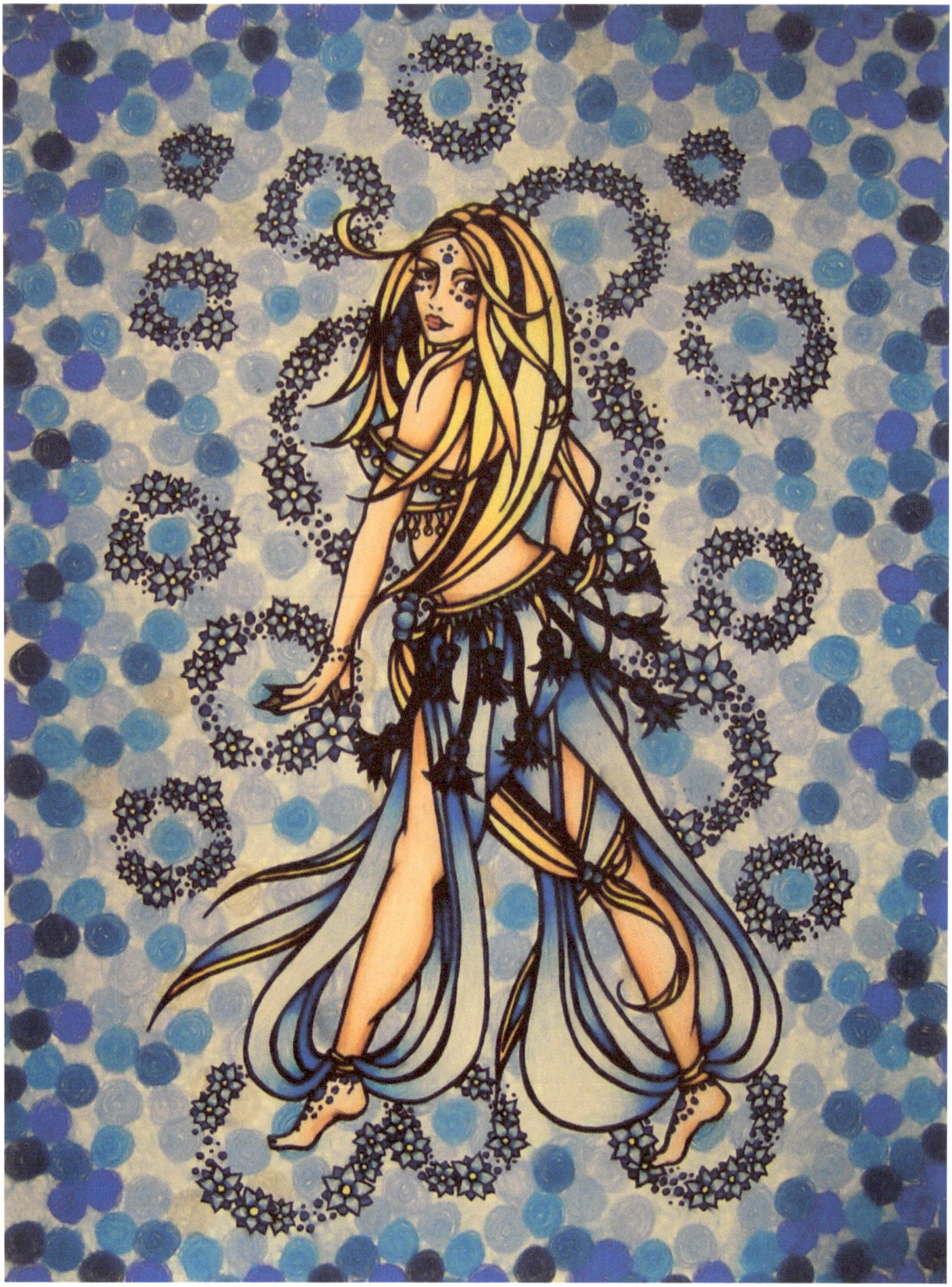

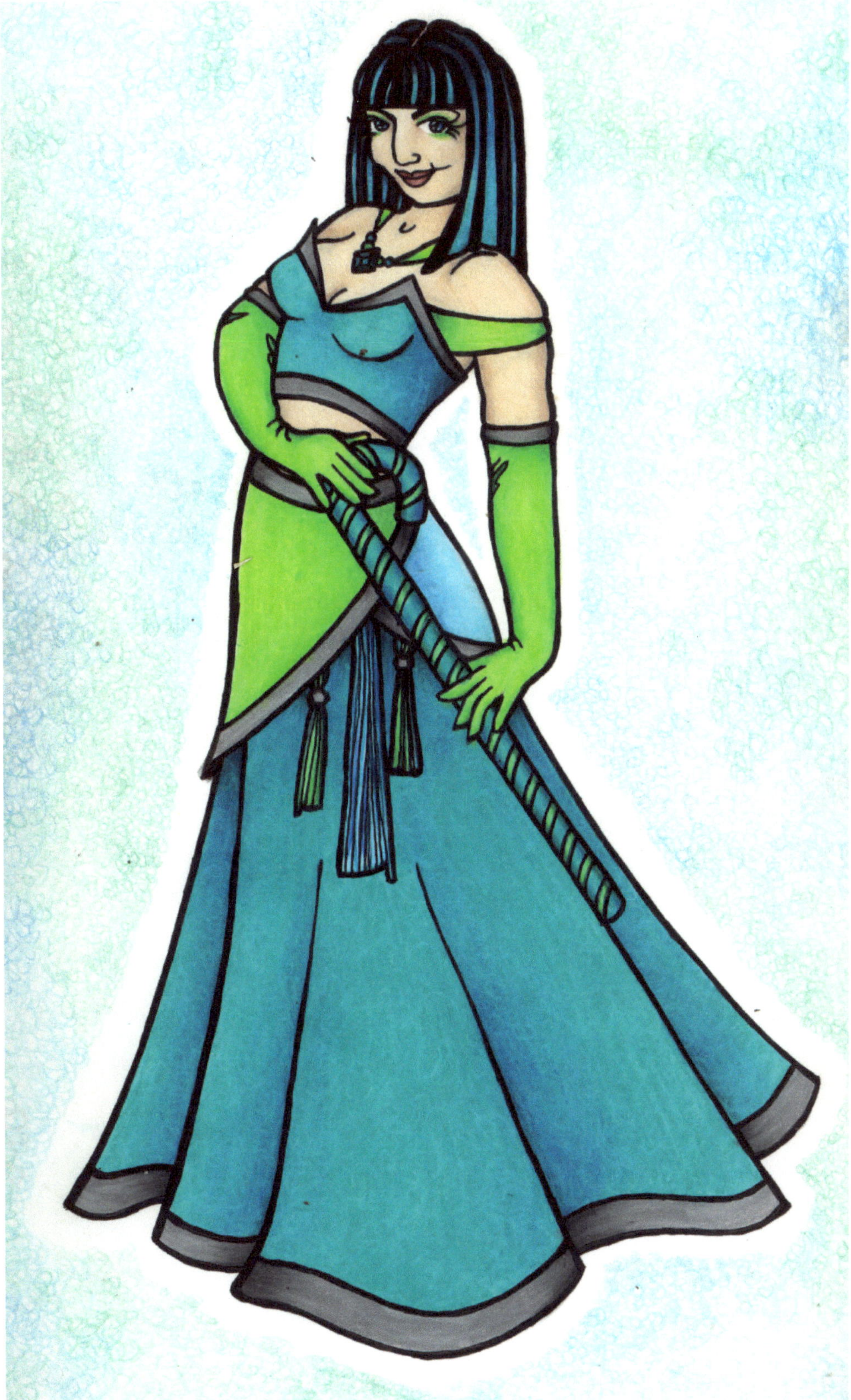

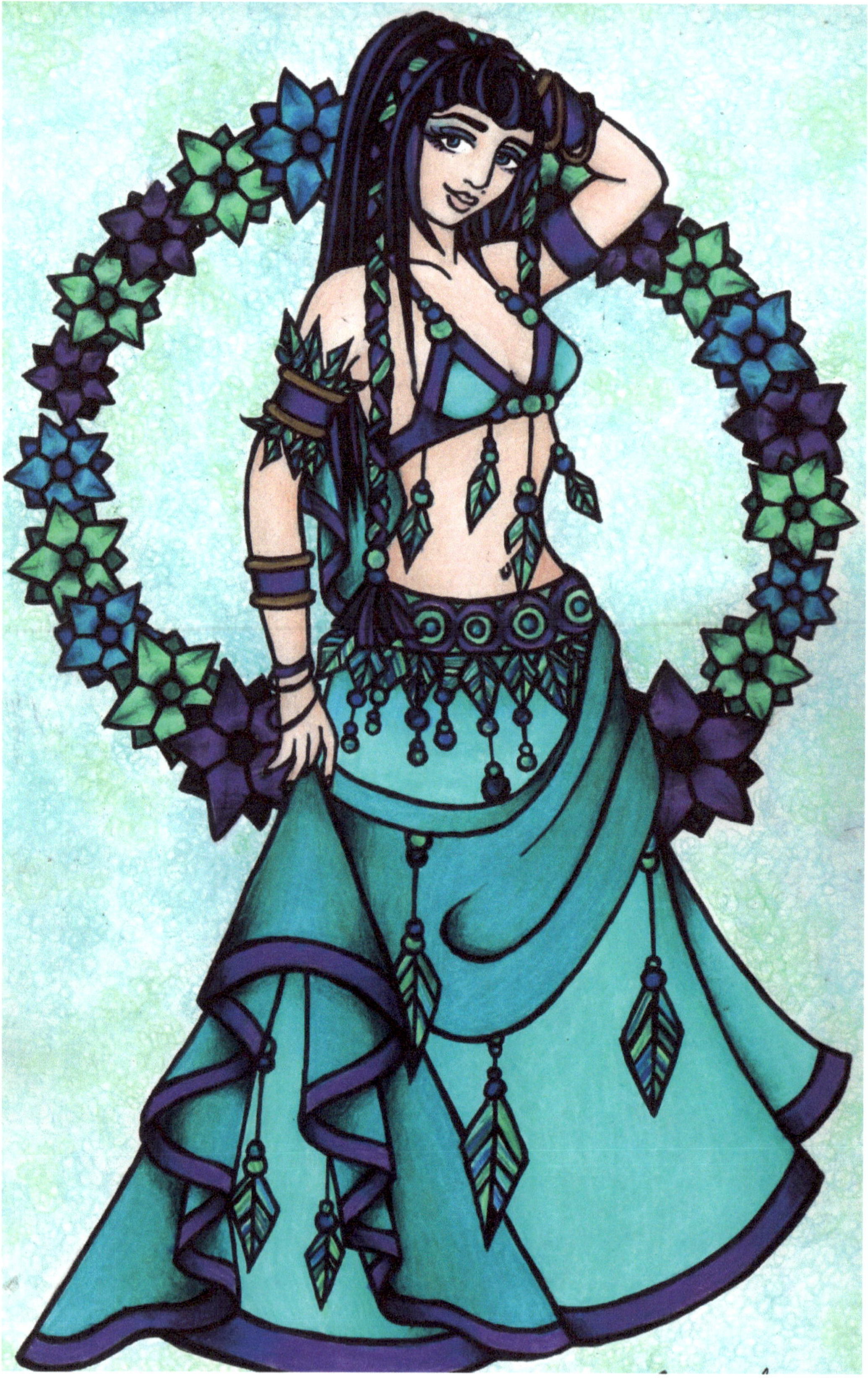

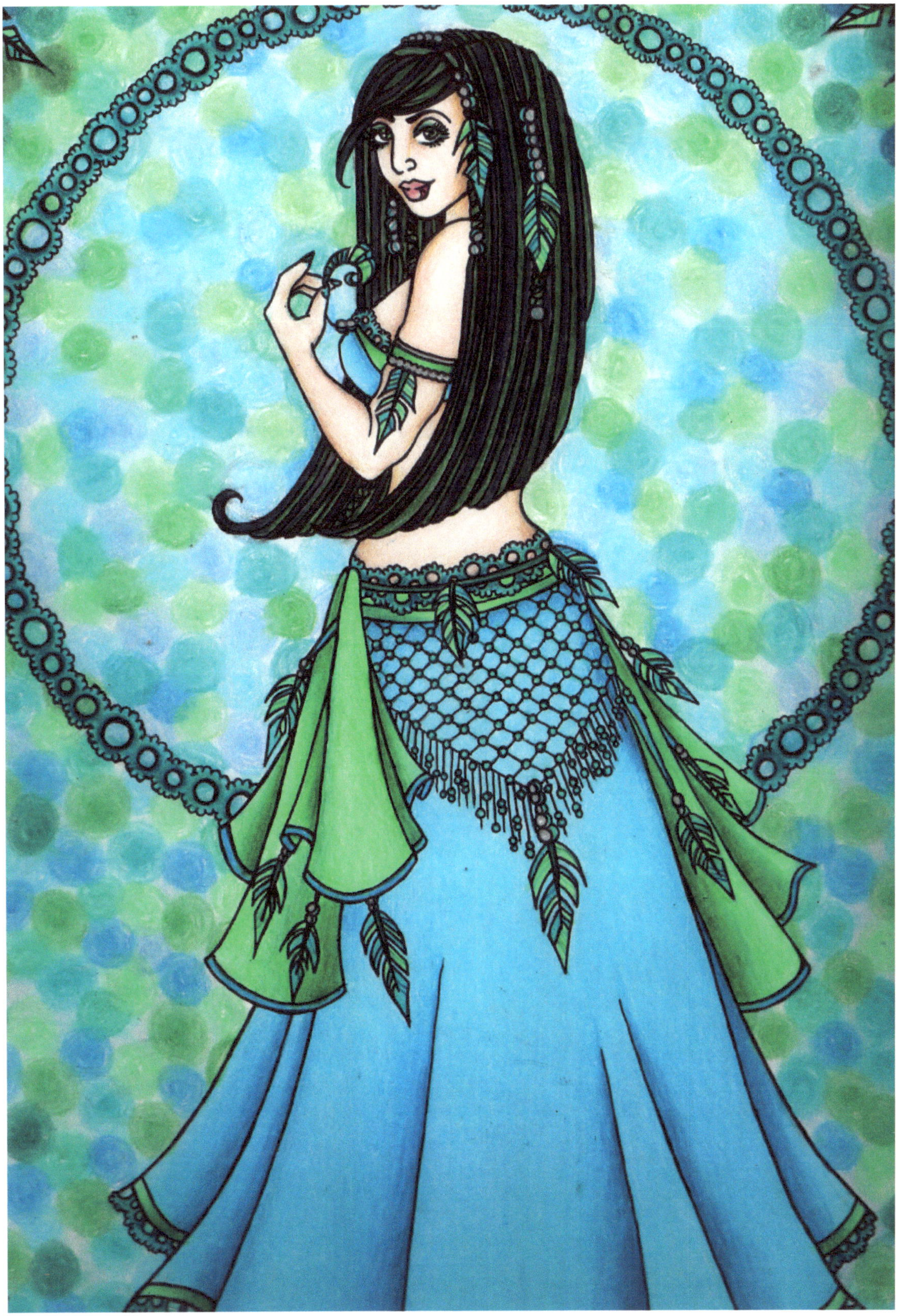

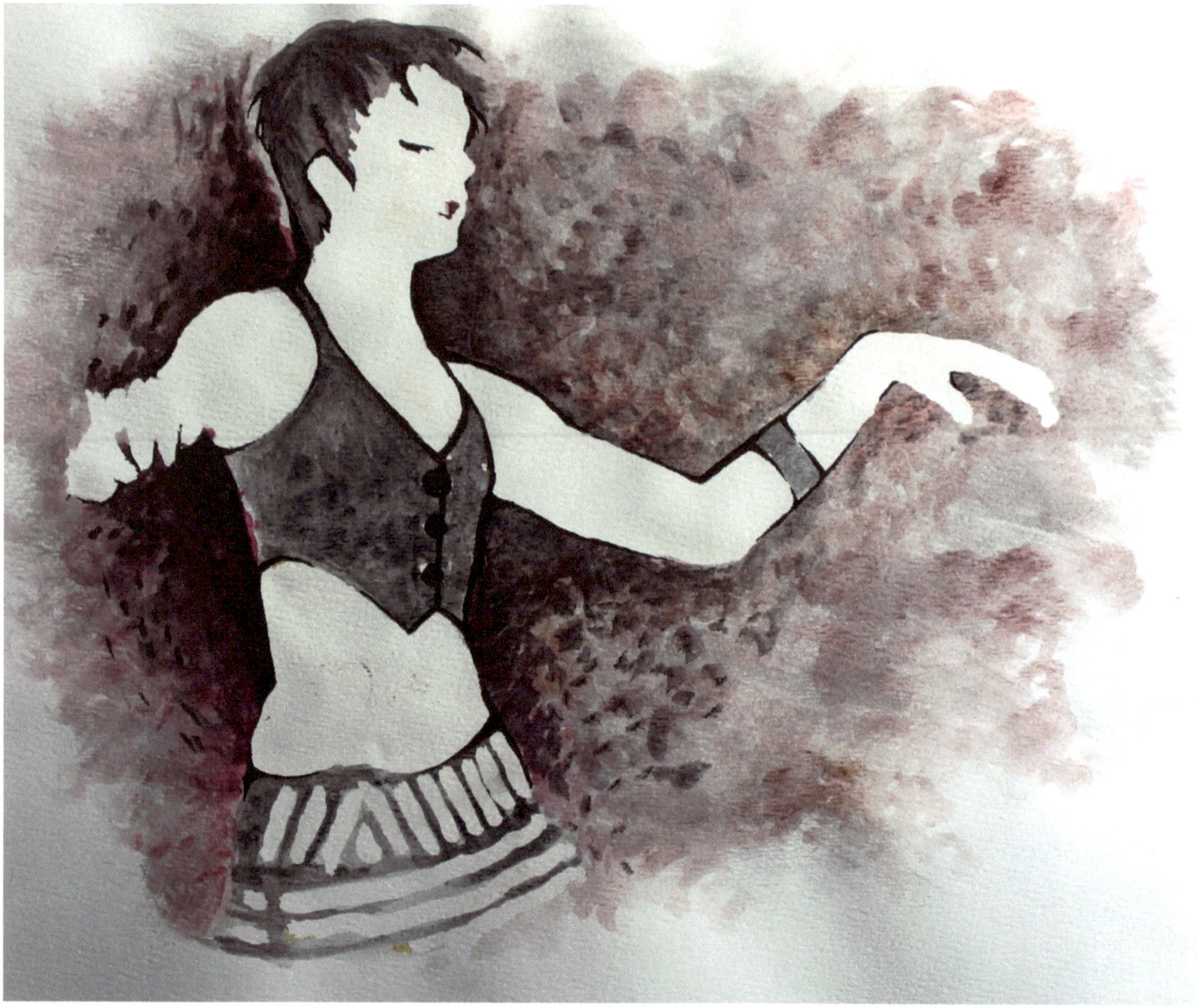

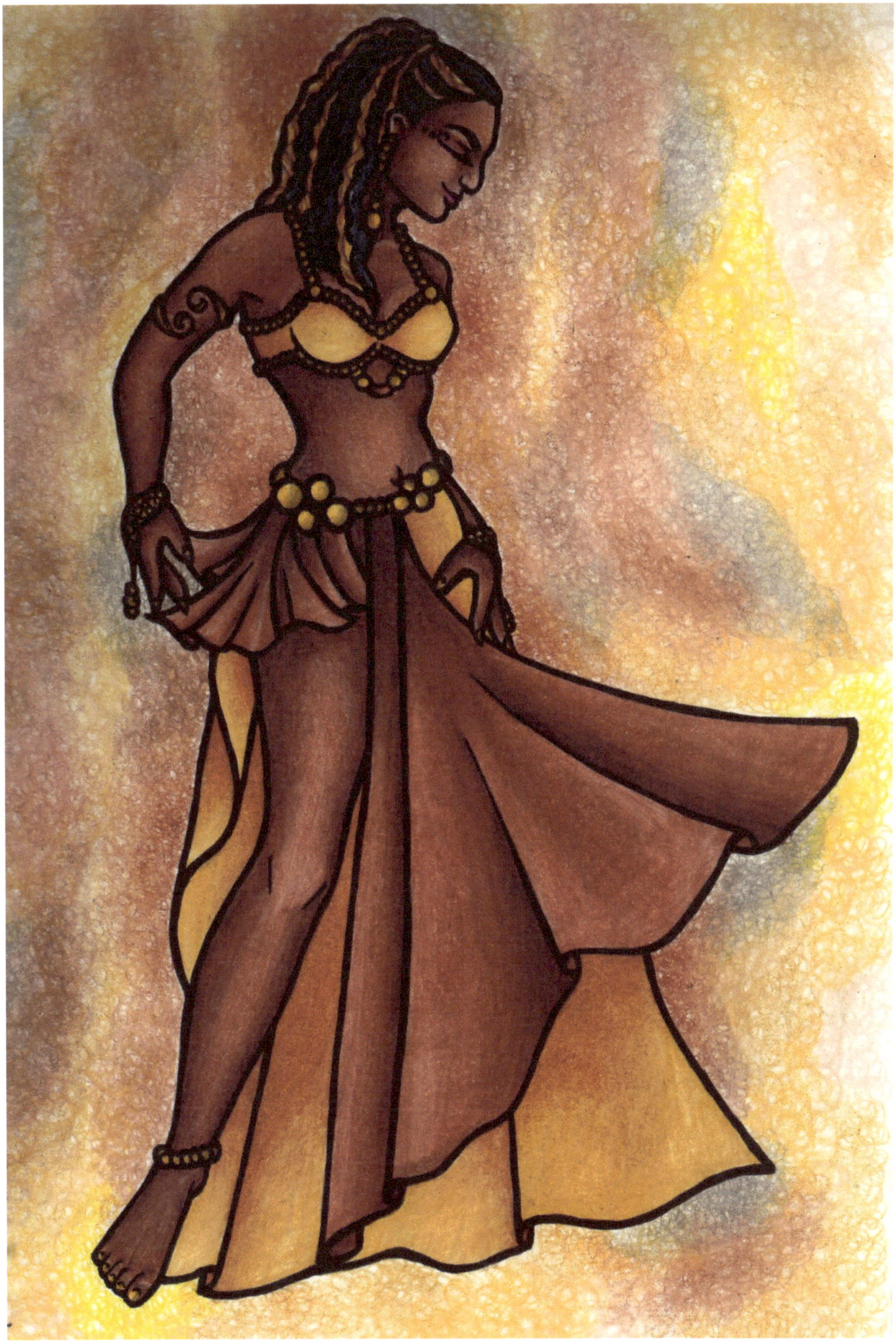

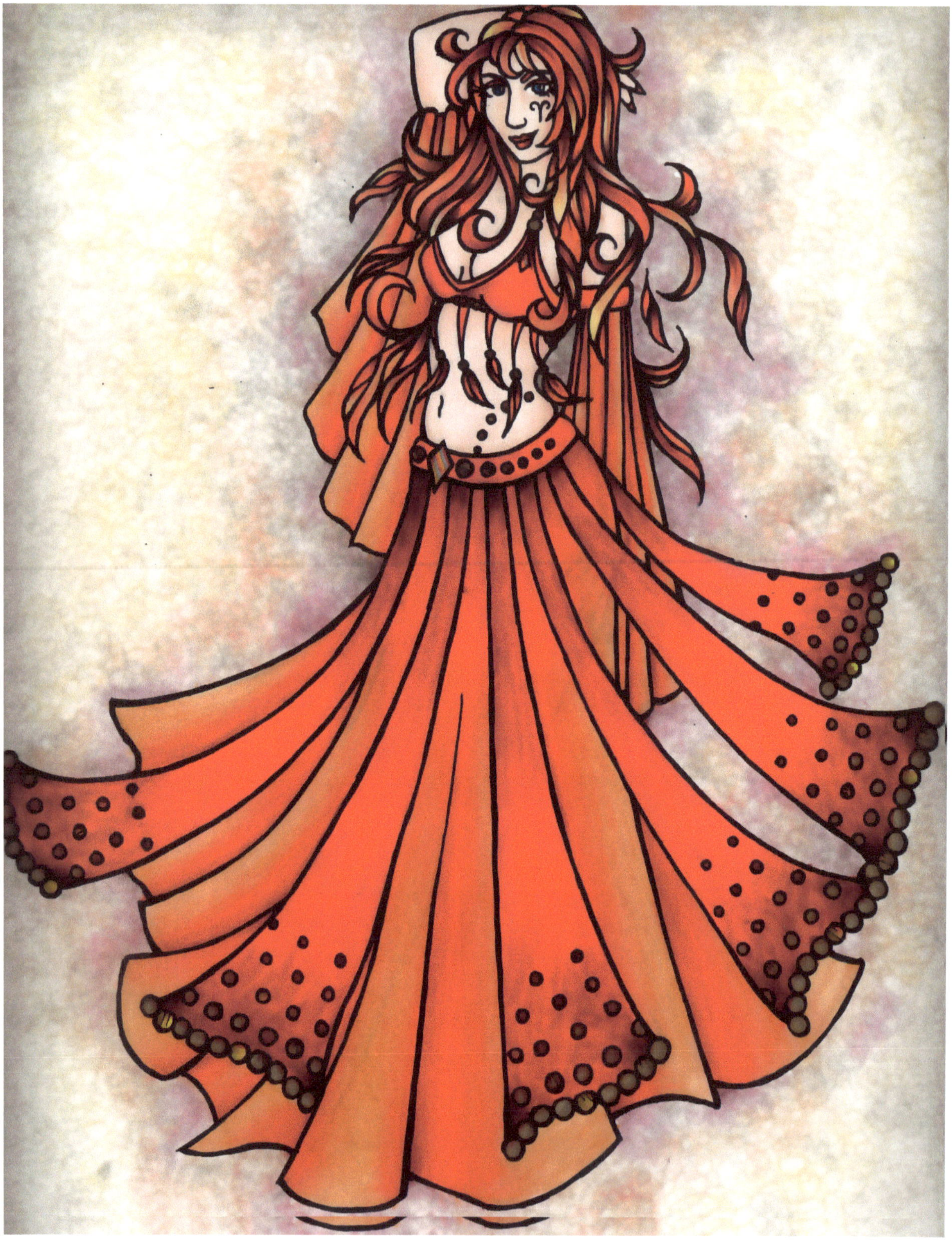

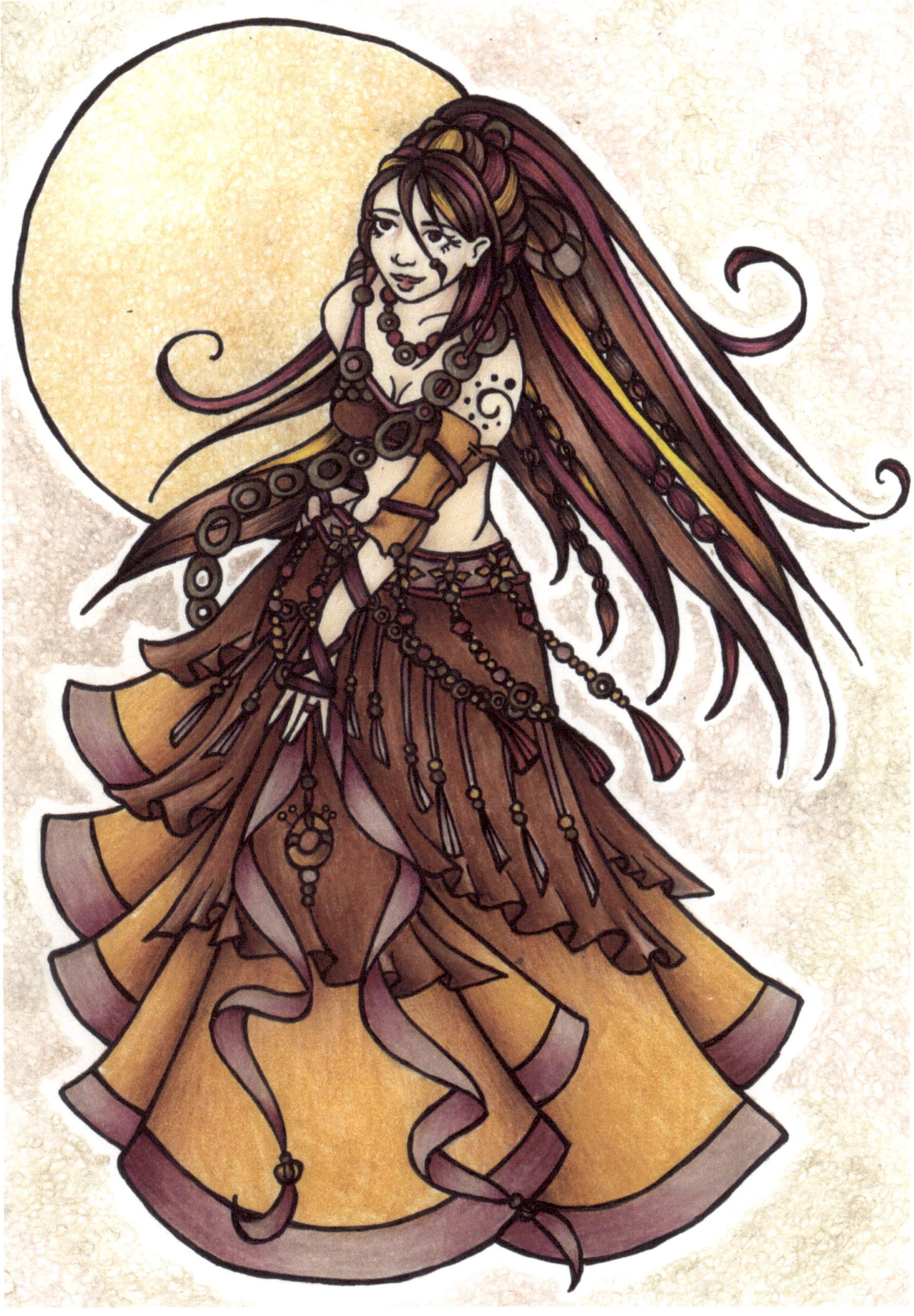

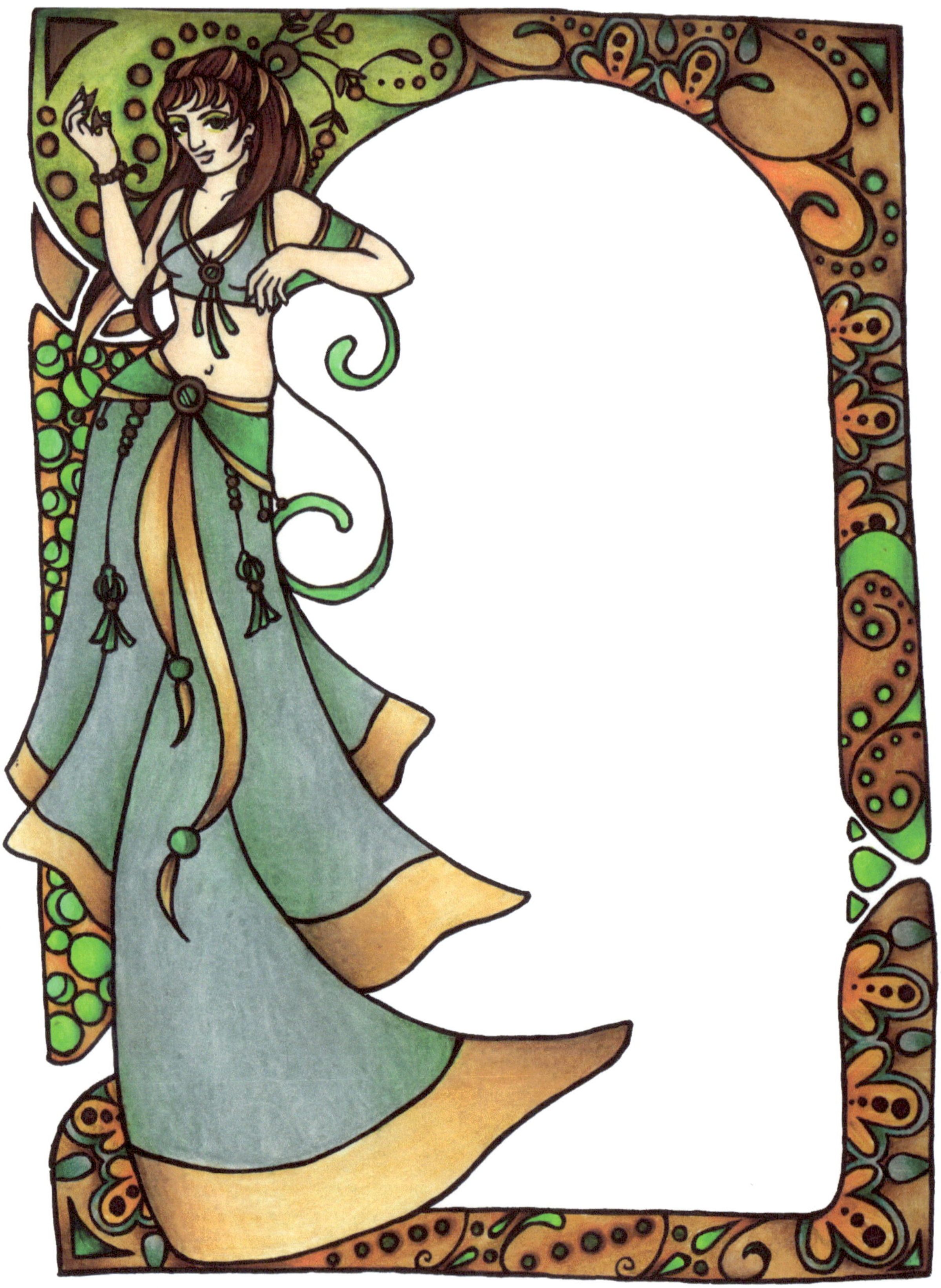

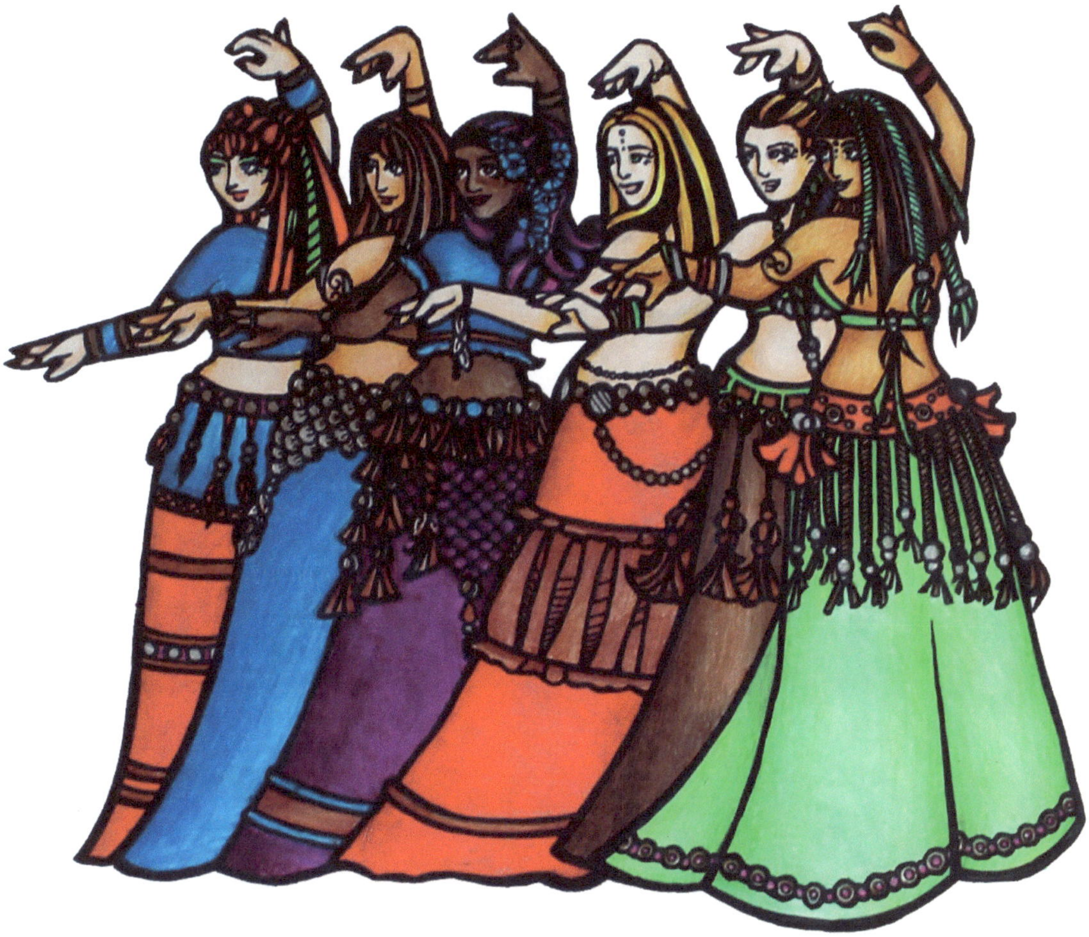

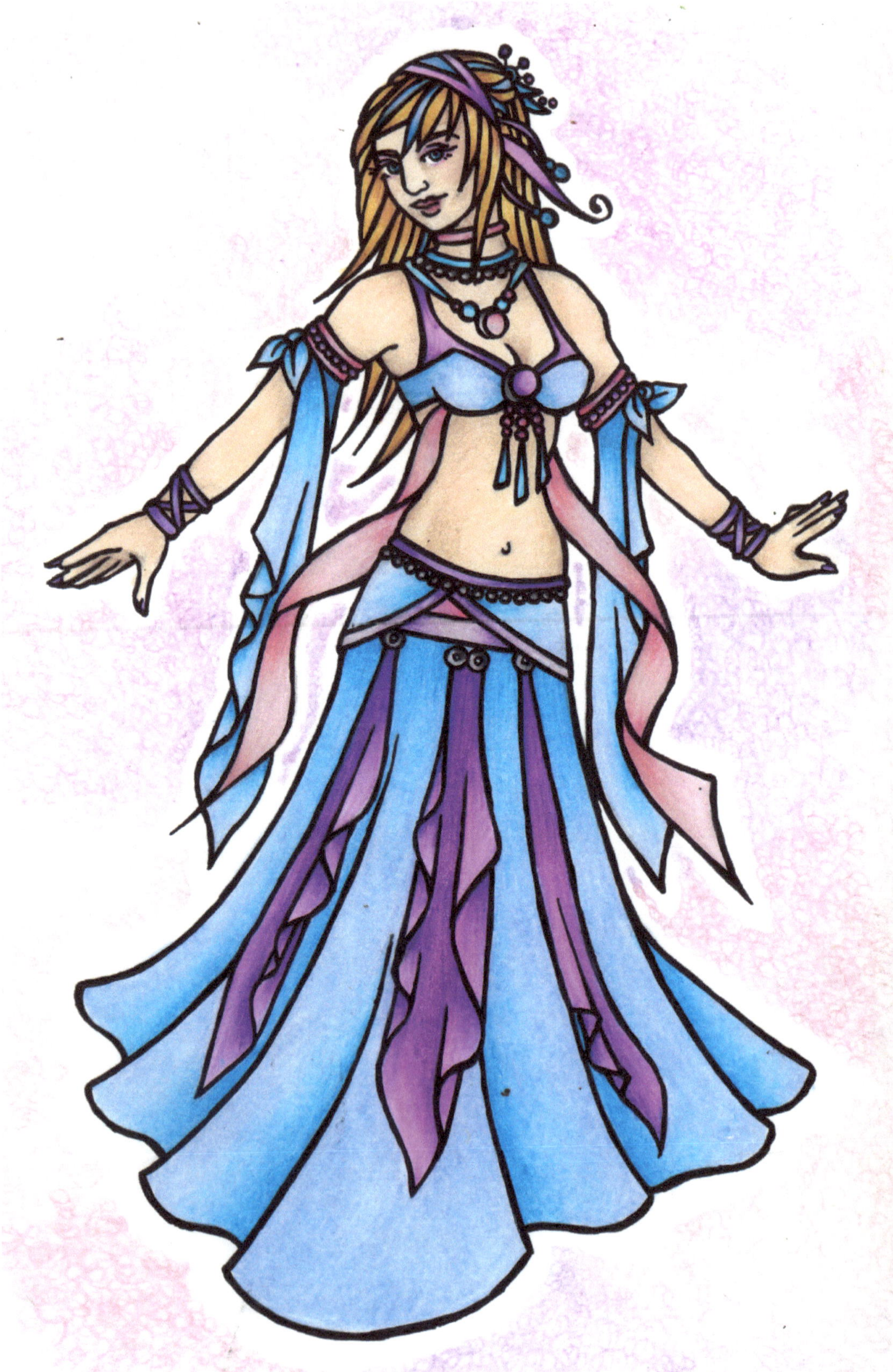

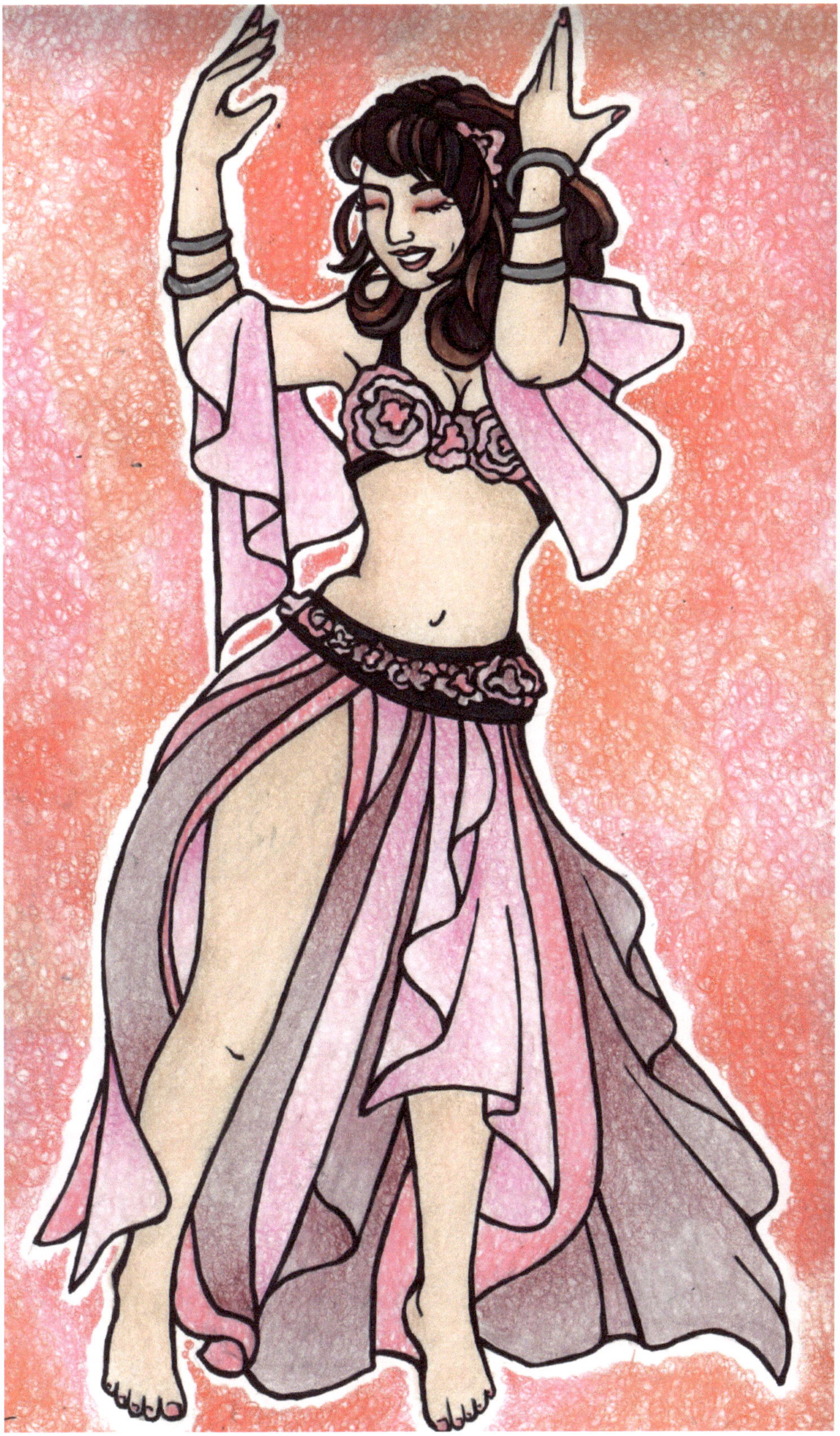

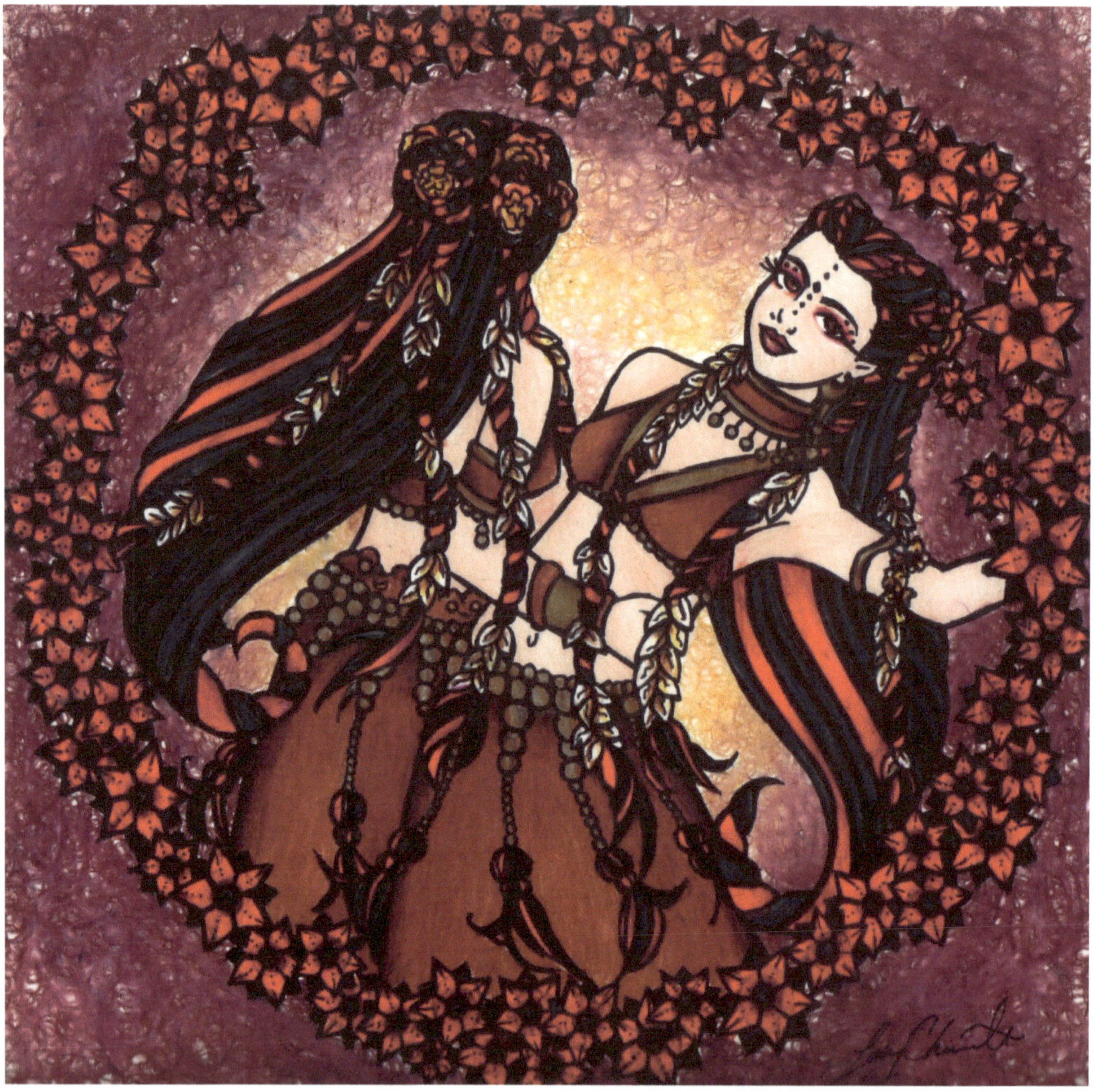

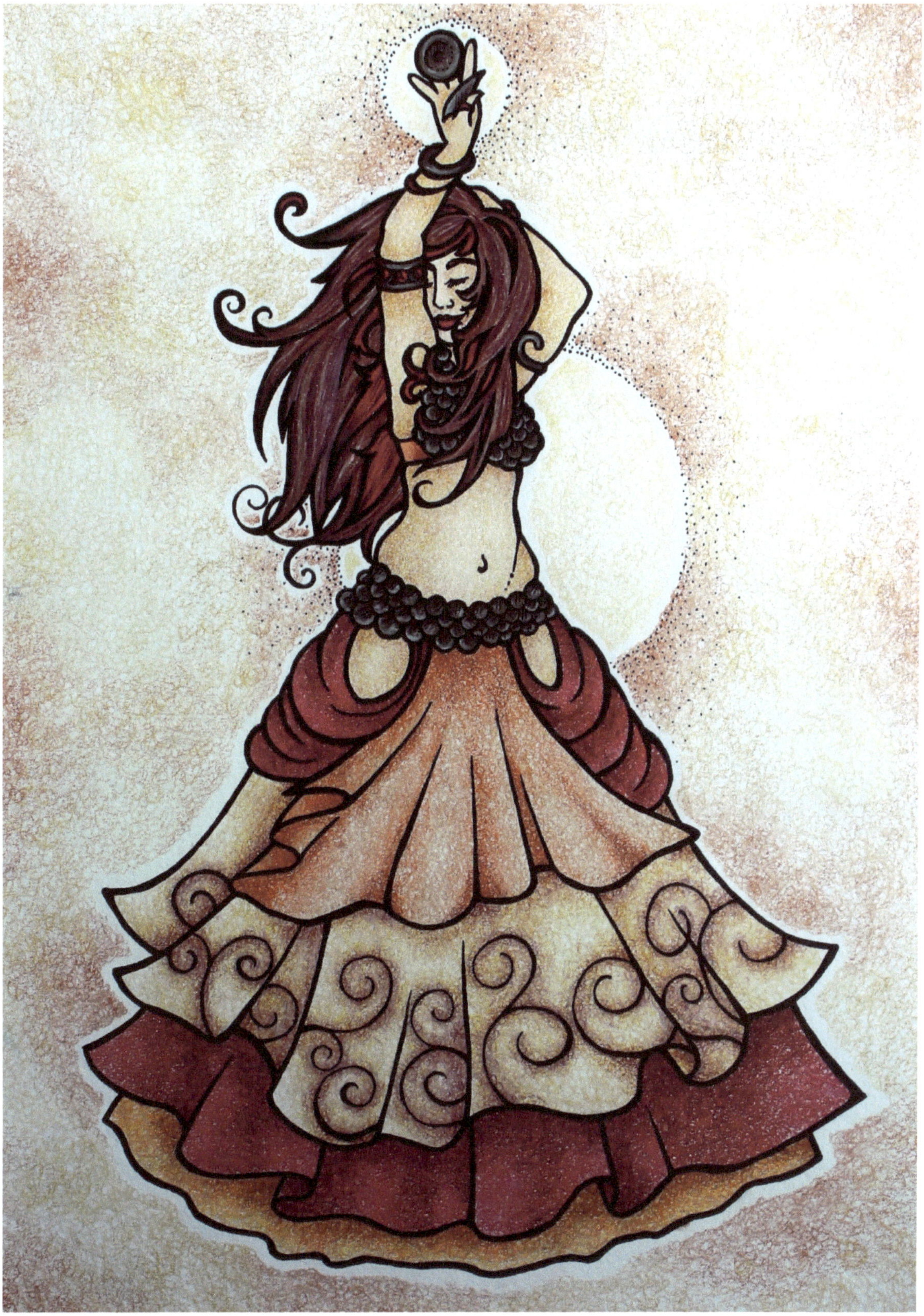

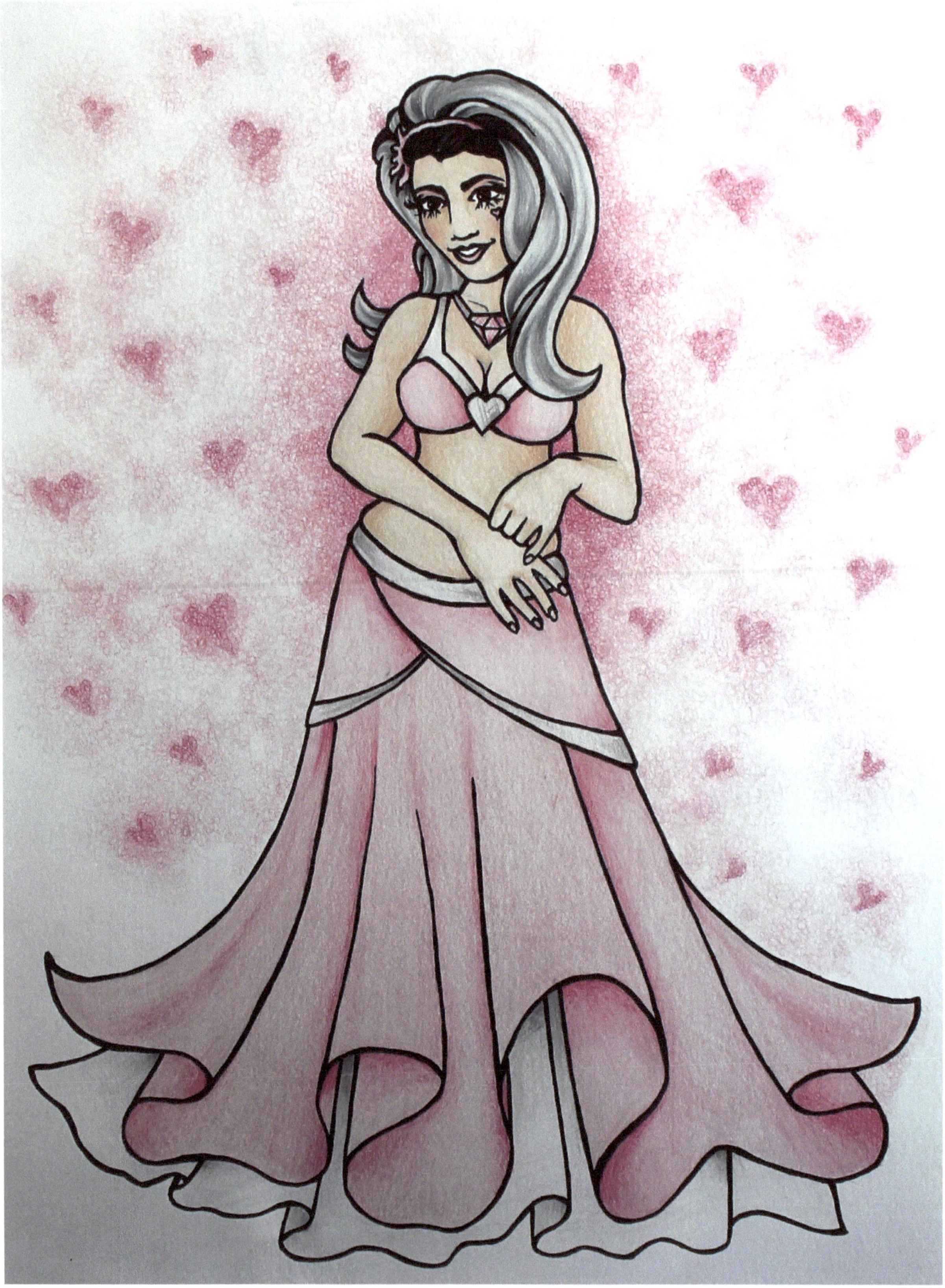

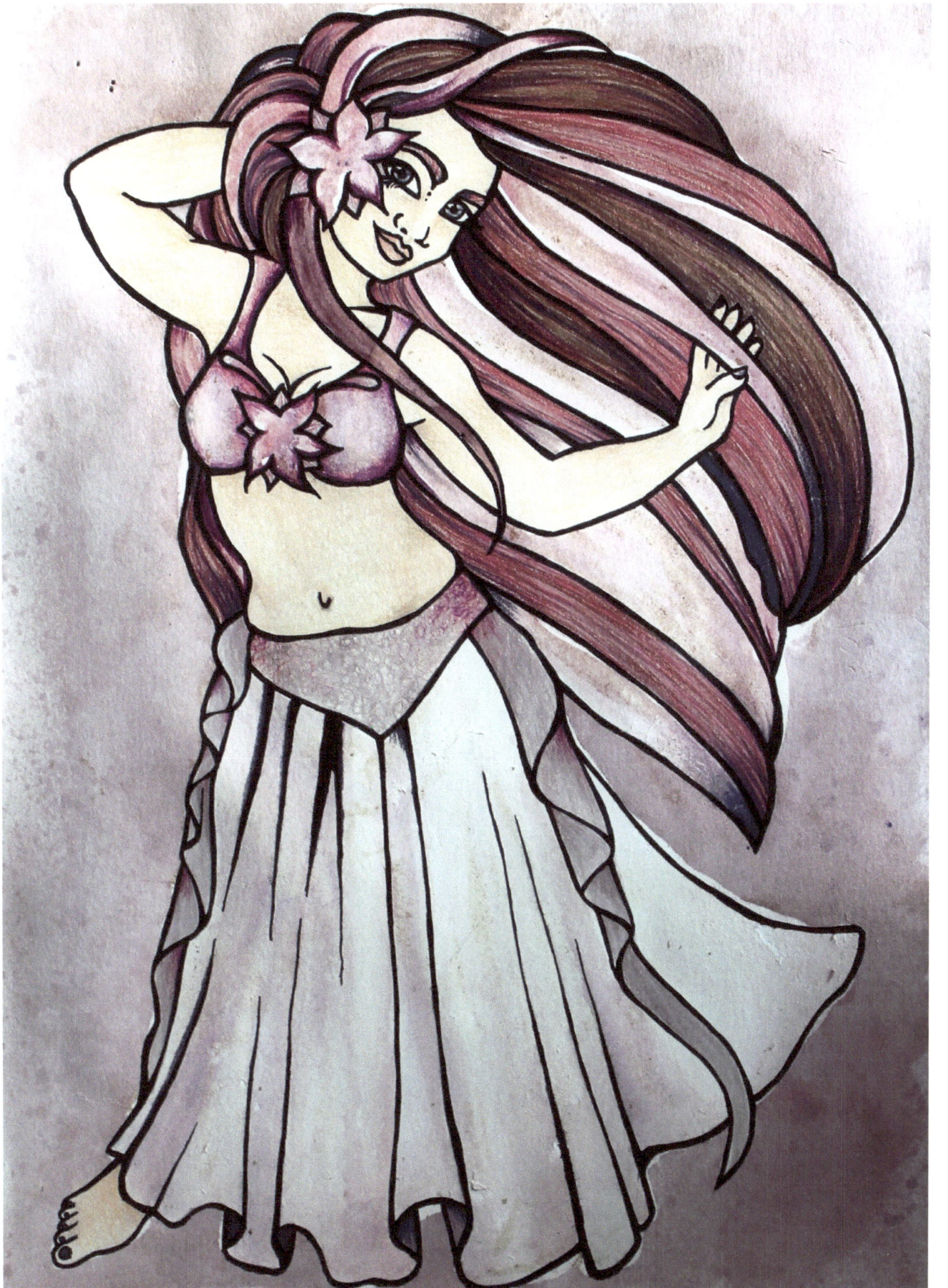

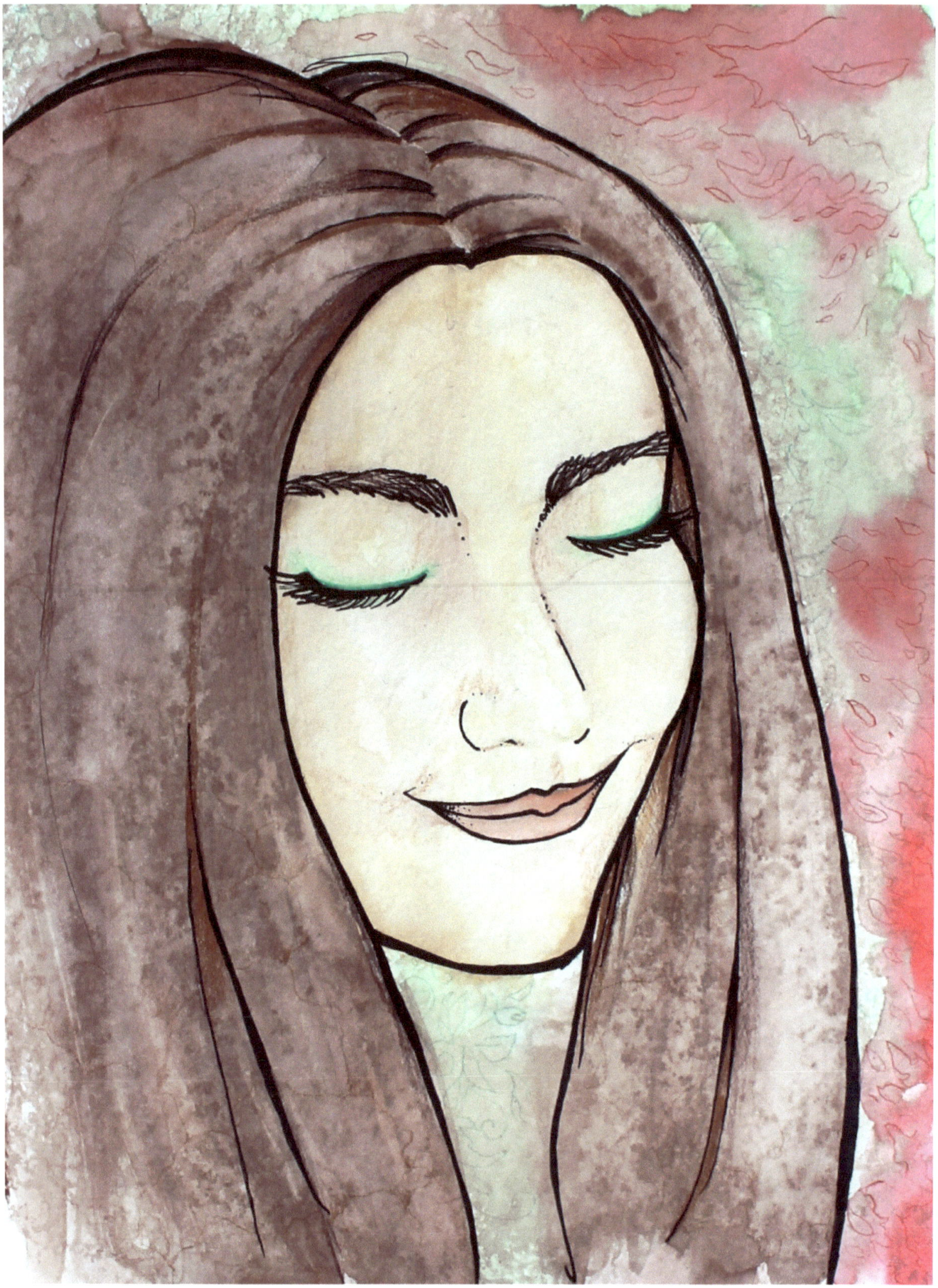

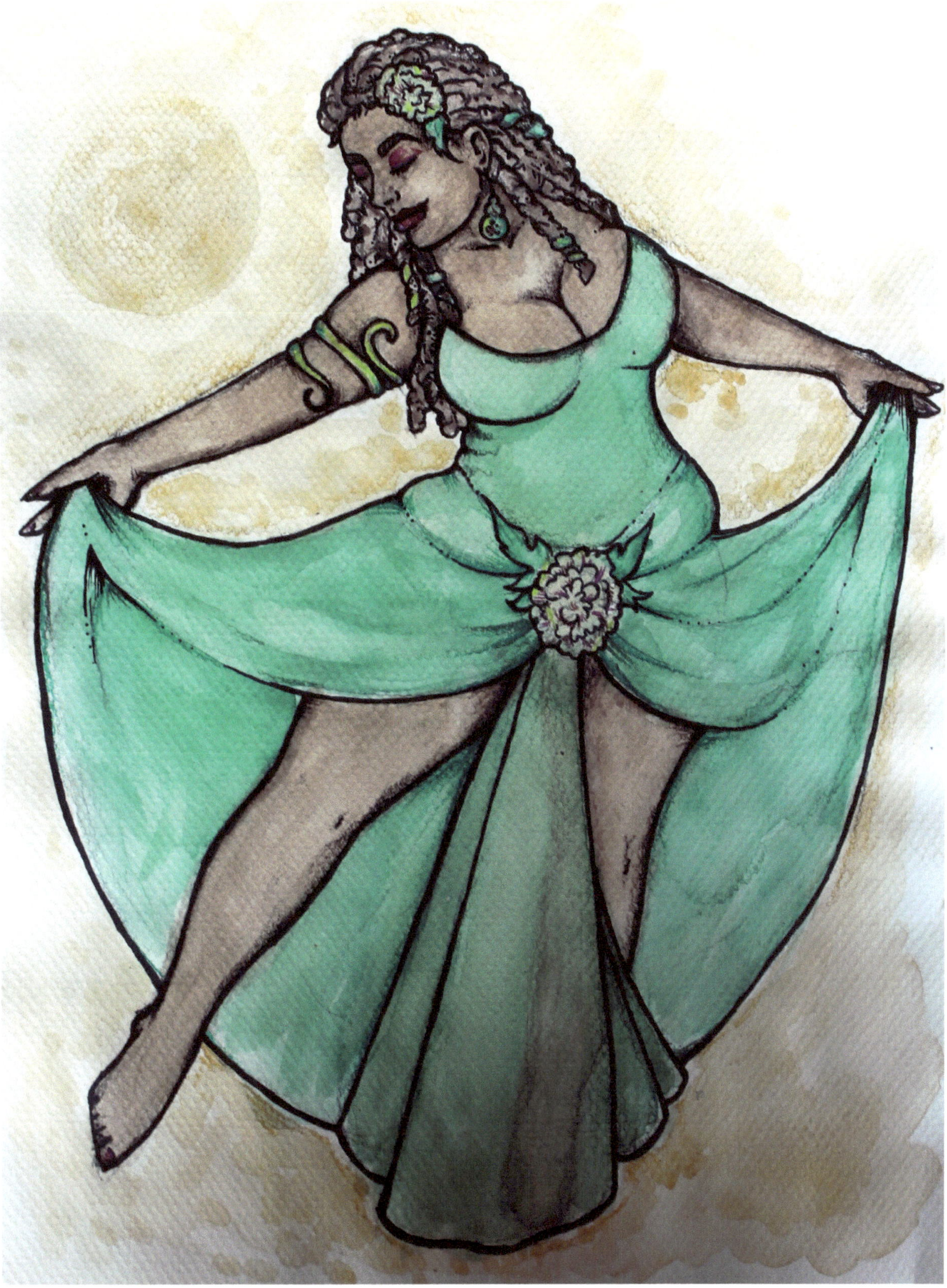

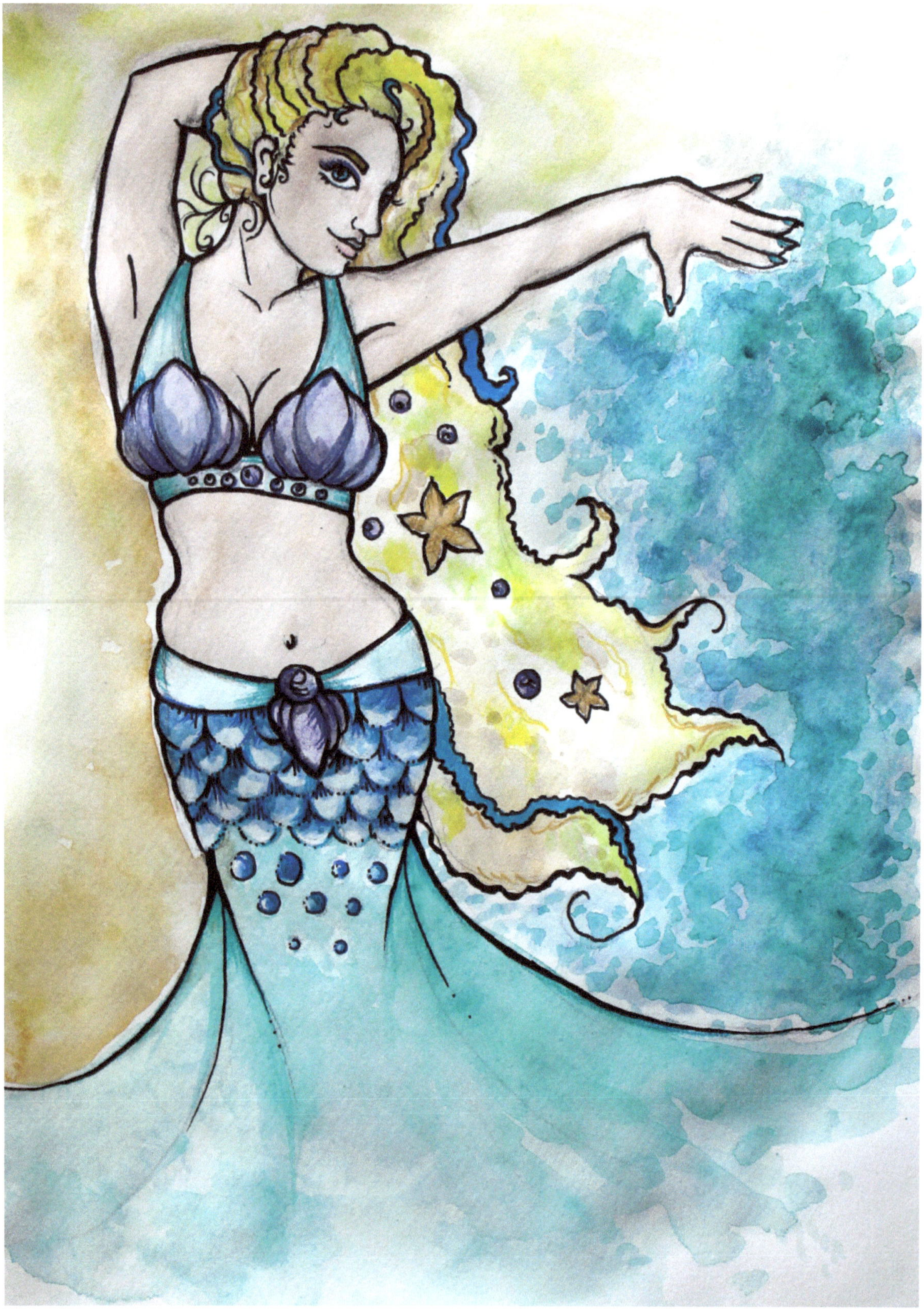

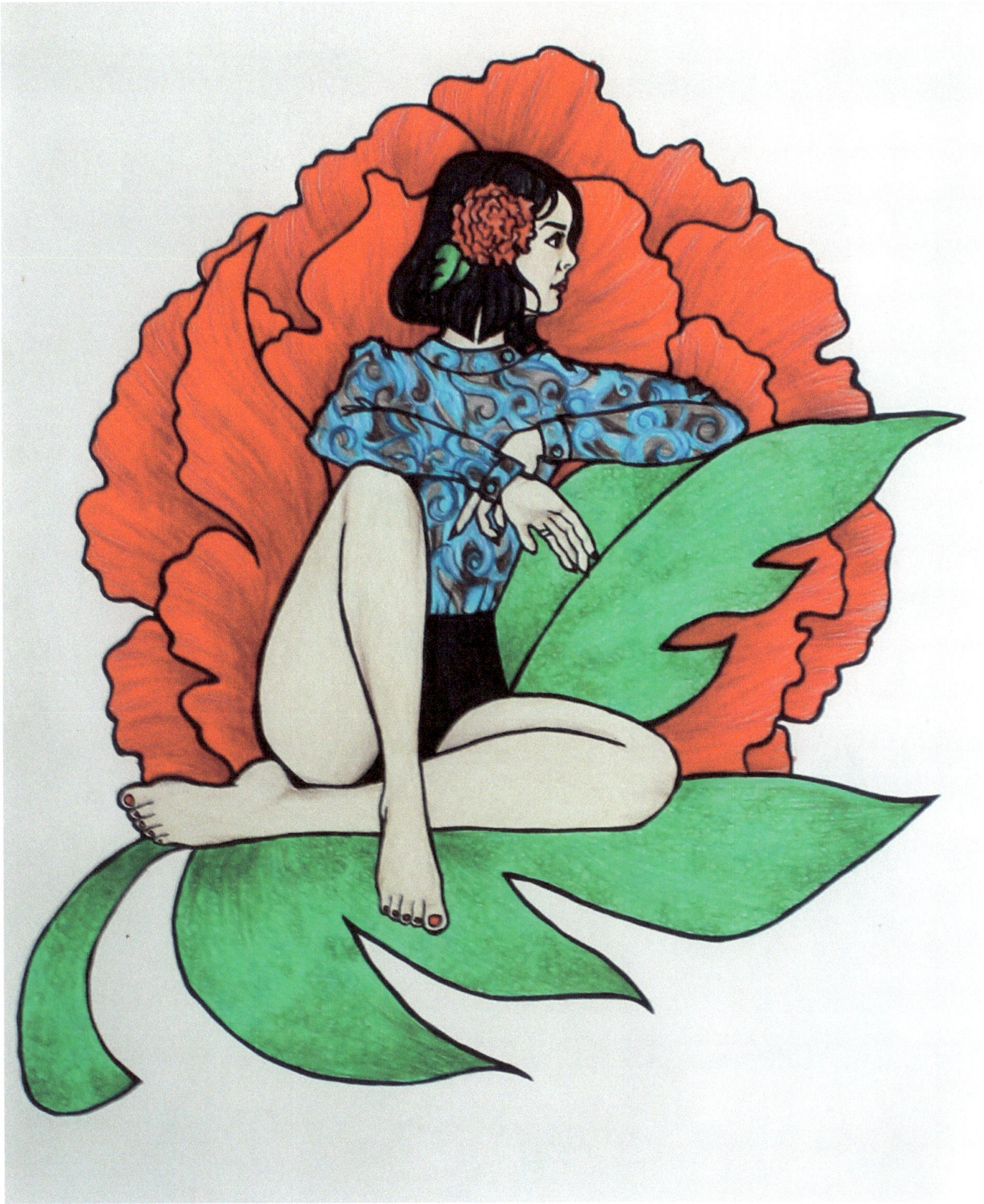

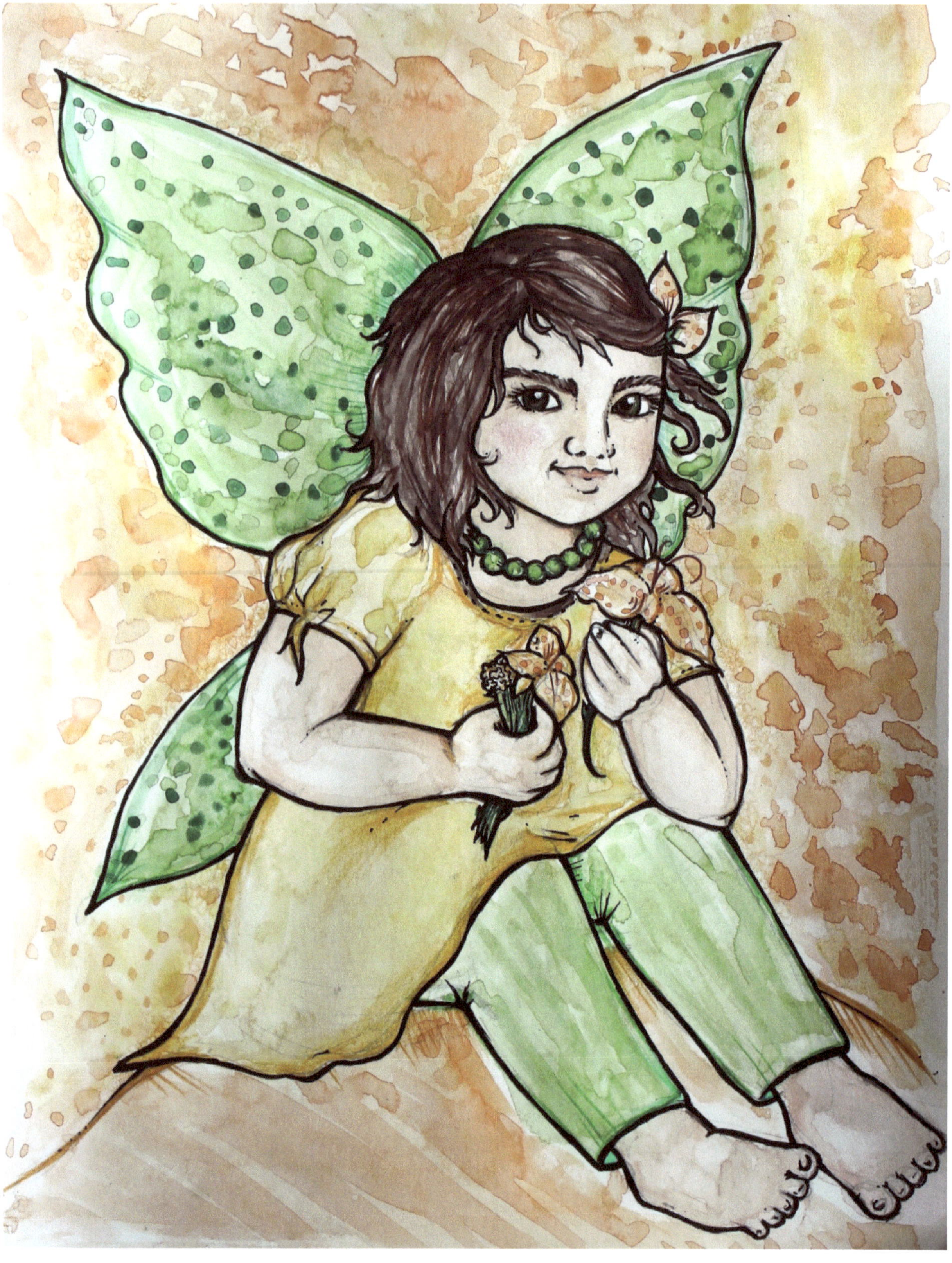

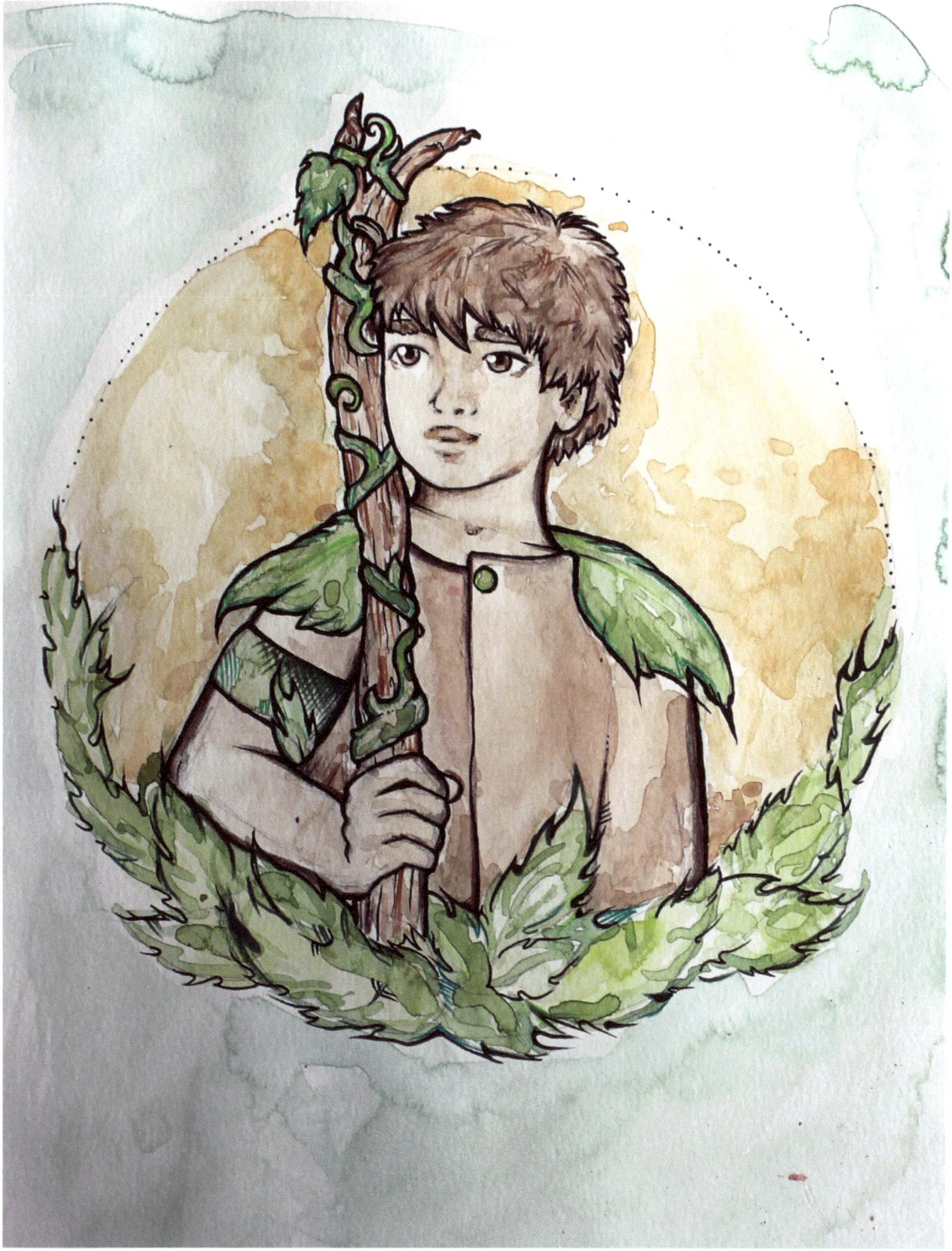

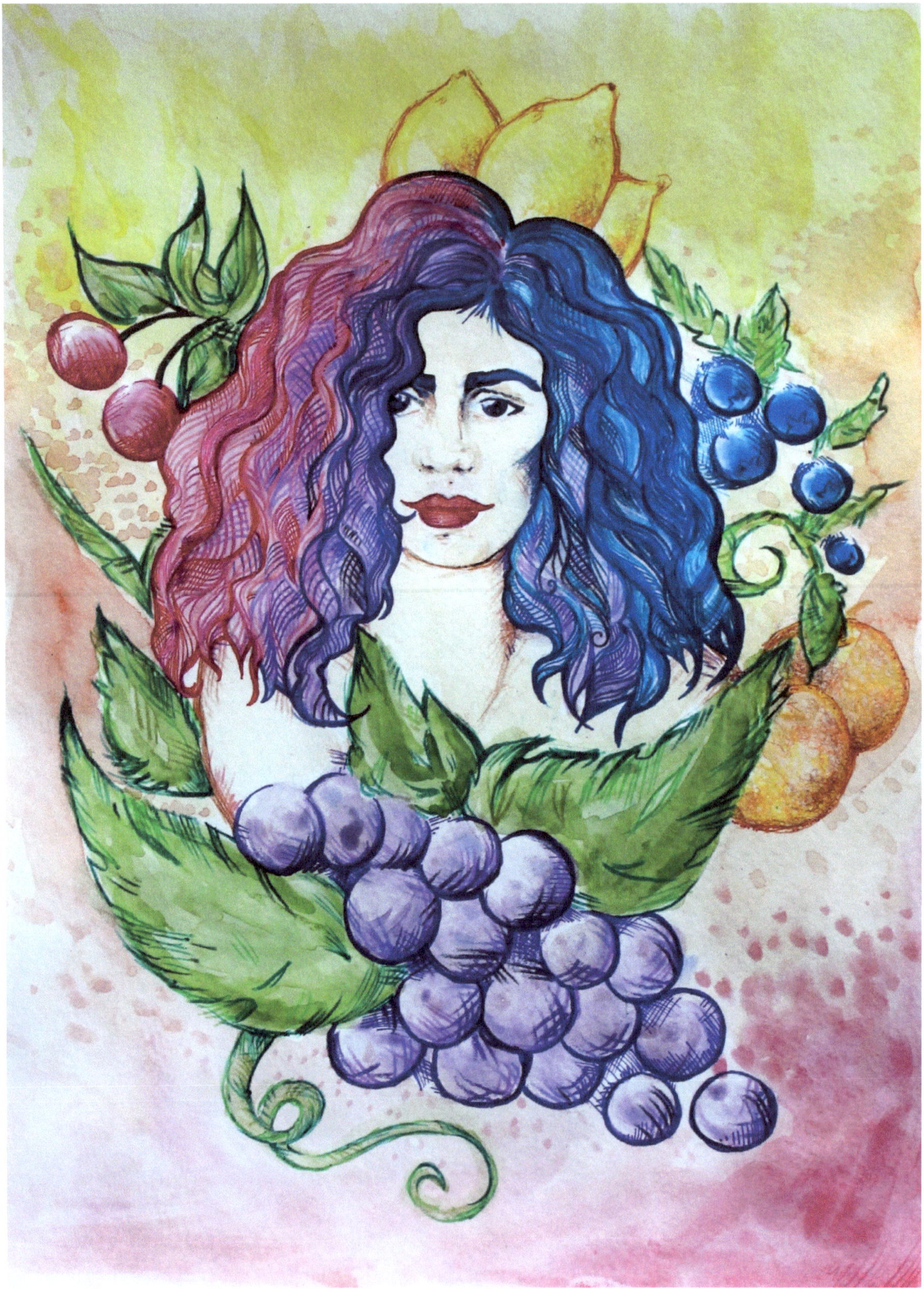

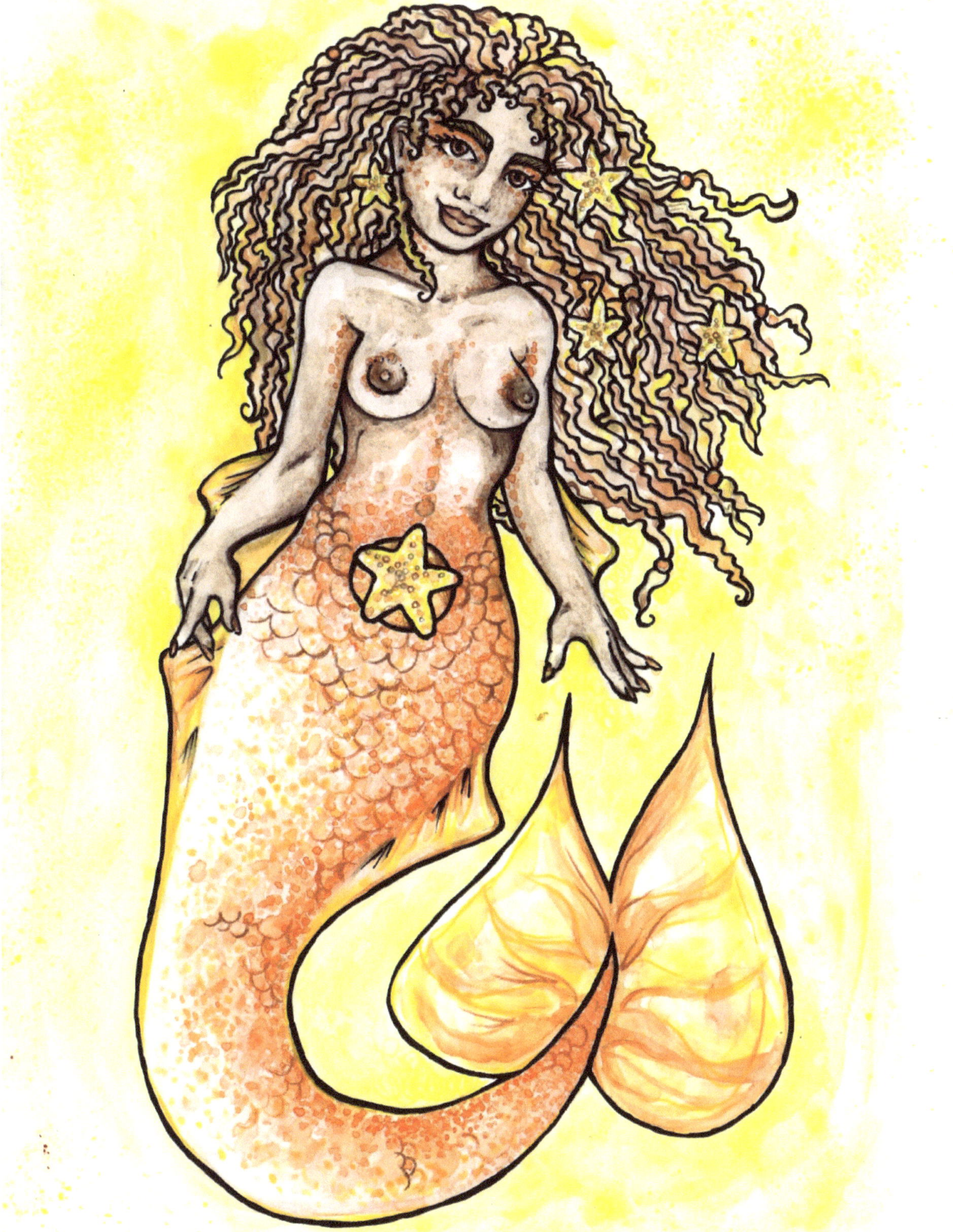

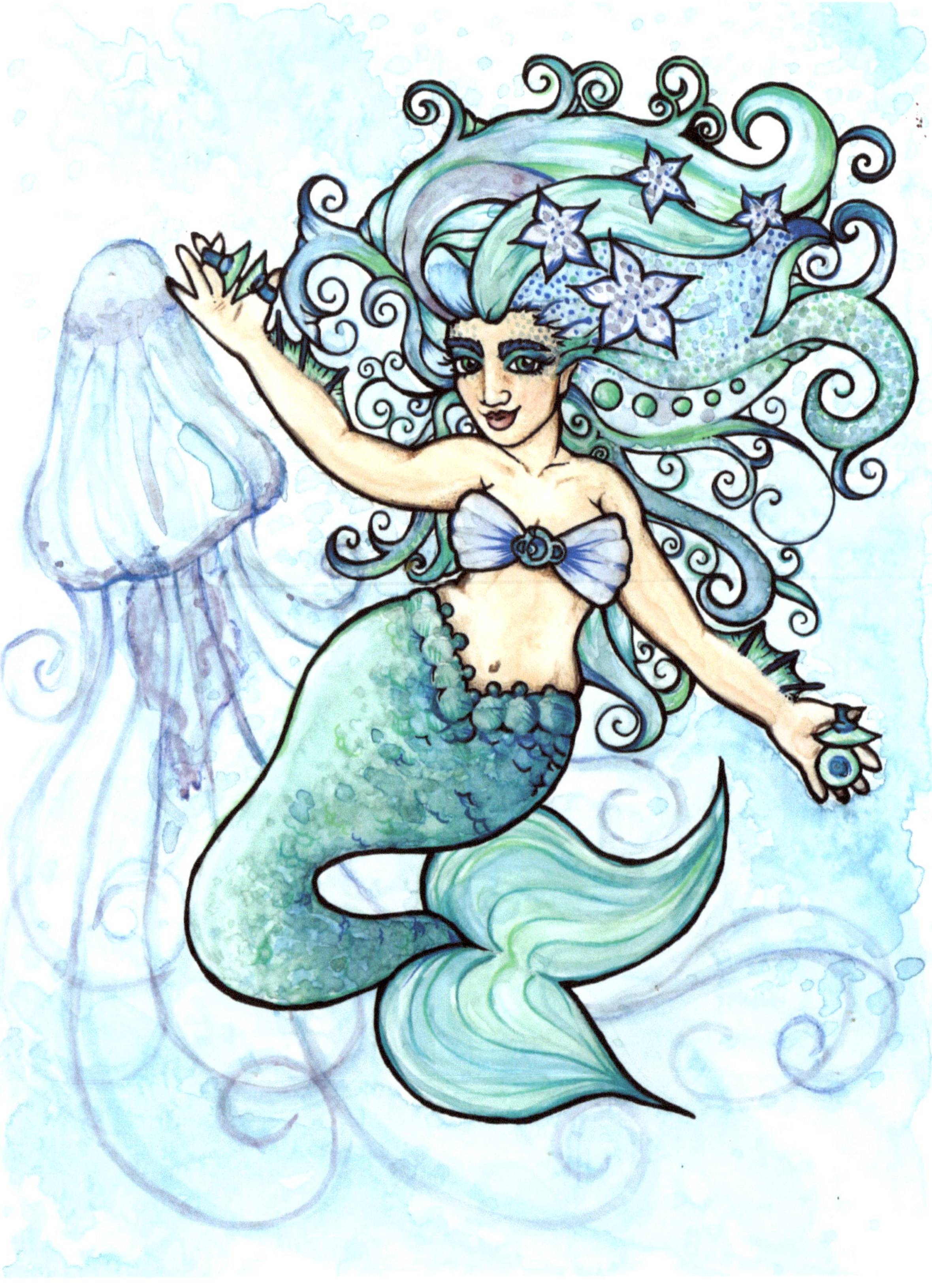

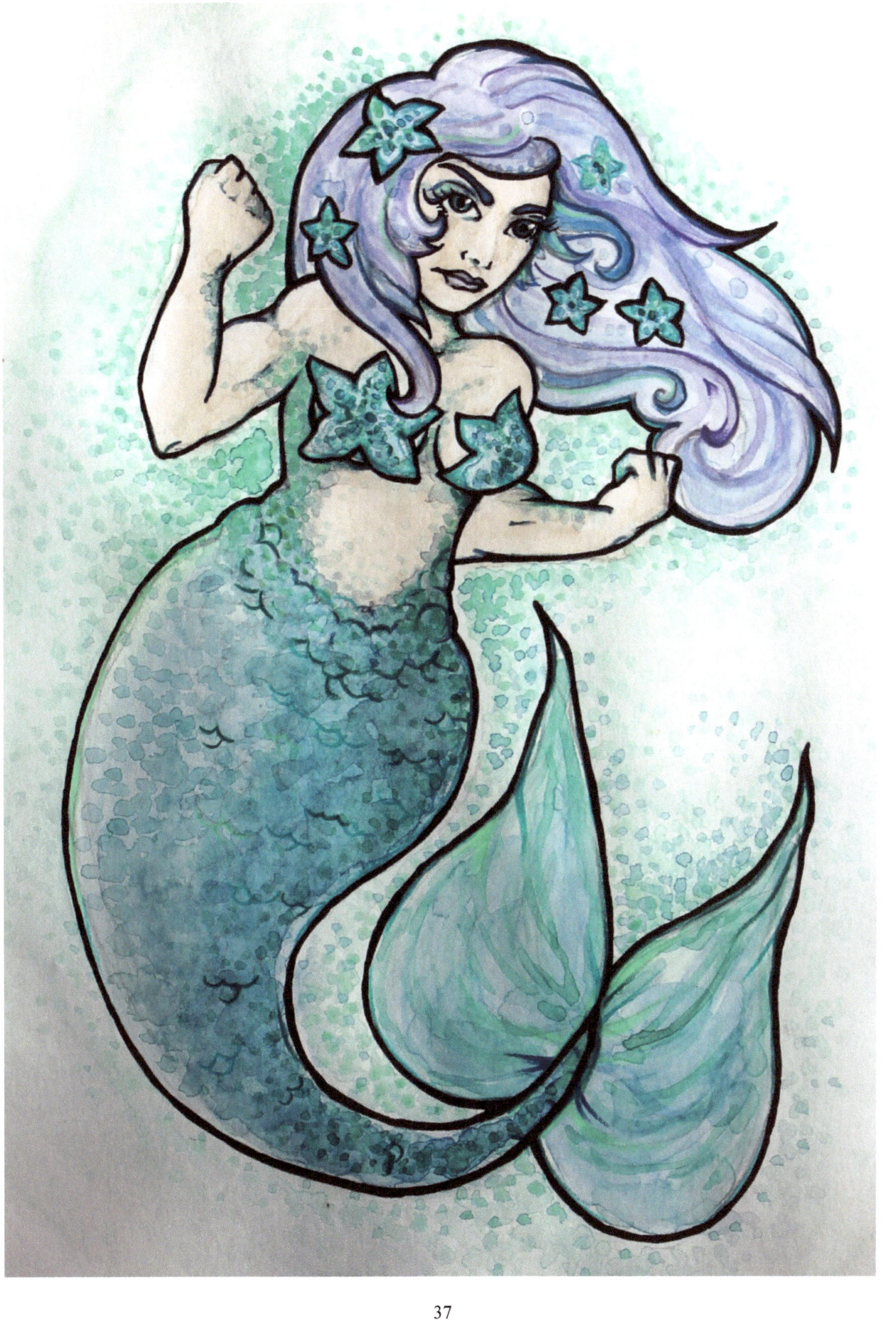

www.ingramcontent.com/pod-product-compliance
Lightning Source LLC
Chambersburg PA
CBHW041318180526
45172CB00004B/1140
* 9 7 8 1 5 2 2 7 5 9 9 8 0 *